Who Am I?

...From Galilee to Jerusalem

A Narrative & Devotional Journey in Lent

By

Rev. Terry Mattson

Copyright © 2015 Rev. Terry Mattson

All rights reserved.

ISBN: 9781520267234

Who Am I?

Rev. Terry Mattson

INTRODUCTION

Who Am I?
...from Galilee to Jerusalem

It began centuries before on a Mount called Sinai, where God revealed to Moses the birth of a nation and her covenant of law. In the wilderness and in Israel God formed his people, whose rebellions and failures God turned into a salvational offering for the whole world, for you and me.

With Jesus and the twelve, we begin our Season of Lent at another Mount, Hermon and in a pagan hideaway near a city called Caesarea Philippi. It was to this mount Jesus called his disciples away, to reflect on his mission and address the question; **Who am I?**

About the En Gedi Nahal David waterfall and Banias cave
It is situated 25 miles north of the Sea of Galilee and at the base of Mt. Hermon at Caesarea Philippi and is the location of one of the largest springs feeding the Jordan River. This abundant water supply has made the area very fertile and was attractive for religious worship in ancient Israel. Numerous temples were built at this city in the Hellenistic and Roman periods

It was to this cavern that many in Israel believed the gods would winter, in the underworld only to be called forth in the Spring with the rituals and offerings (often sexual in nature) which would entice the gods to favor the land, to make it fertile once again. Hence, by the time of Jesus they became known as "The Gates of Hades".

Some scholars believe it was to this place that Jesus called into being his church as he declared that *"on this rock I will build my church, and the **gates of Hades** will not overcome it"* (Matthew 16:18).

Rev. Terry Mattson

Pastor Emeritus,

West Seattle Church of the Nazarene

07/16/15

UNDERSTANDING THIS BOOK

If this writing has any value for you it will be in the dialogue between you, the Spirit of God, and the Church.

These stories/writings are drawn from my own imagination, creating moments in John the Apostle's journey with Jesus only as I envision them; moments that certainly did not happen as described. Often, something very much like them probably did happen. At the very least, I hope you will discover the Biblical setting, the feel of the times in which John lived and something of his own passion as the beloved of Jeshua and of the early Church.

These writings express my own thoughts, feelings, and ideas often in response to reflections on writings from a book called "Turn My Mourning into Dancing", written by Henri Nouwen. Henri Nouwen was an ordained priest and gifted teacher, author, lecturer and spiritual mentor. Having taught at several universities, worldwide, he completed his ministry as pastor of the L'Arche Community of Daybreak in Toronto, Canada. His reflections came, in no small part, from this season of his life serving a community of the disabled.

You can purchase "Turn My Mourning Into Dancing" by Henri Nouwen at Amazon.com (either in Kindle or Paper Back). Go to:

https://www.amazon.com/Turn-My-Mourning-into-Dancing/dp/0849945097/ref=sr_1_15?ie=UTF8&qid=1483078345&sr=8-15&keywords=henri+nouwen

I have kept the focus of my reflections on the last journey of Jesus and the twelve from Mt. Hermon in northern Galilee to Jerusalem, moving from Ash Wednesday toward Jerusalem and the final week of passion toward Easter Sunday. I believe you will find yourself within this extraordinary journey of the Twelve from Galilee to Jerusalem. I hope you will ask yourself anew 'Who Am I?' as you enter into the first disciples wrestling with who Jesus is.

The Faith given is both personal and social, human and Divine, always. Therefore, readings from Scripture and the imagined story are interwoven, so that you and The Spirit who inspires The Story and writes it into the imagination of your heart, can reflect together.

To that end you are given for each week of the next seven a:

- ➢ Psalm per week (to be read each day of the week), and;
- ➢ Quote of the week (to meditate upon), and;

- ➤ Selected Scripture for each day, and;
- ➤ Reflections and questions on the scriptures, imagined stories and my devotional thoughts.

You are encouraged to create a journal, titled "Who Am I?" and note in it your own feelings, insights, prayers, confessions, praises and conversations with God which you may wish to keep and review at a later time.

Quotations from other authors will be in italics.

DEDICATION

I want to present this book to Joetta, my lady, who in so many ways walks inside a life of service and disappointment, but with dignity and grace. I have cheated her at every turn; in ministry, money, time and heart as I have spent what must have seemed an eternity asking of myself... "Who am I?" I am sure she has more than once wondered, "who she was" within the journey of our life together.

I have never had to wonder at 'who' she is or 'whose' she is. She is a devout follower and lover of Jesus. Like the disciples of old she will follow him wherever life with Jesus takes her. She reflects daily before the Word and loves beautifully her children, extended family and the Church of Jesus.

She has made possible the redemptive and cross economic and cultural mission in which we are engaged, by loving presence and economic sacrifice.

She is a gifted musician serving in worship while increasingly feeling the pain of a debilitating disease, affecting her hands and joints.

Joetta is wise and intuitive; her speech is captive precisely because of wisdom. Honor follows her because she follows honor!

Beyond that she is expressive in love through food. Weather our home was filled with friends, neighbors, parishioners or the homeless she delighted in presenting a crafted meal that vanquishes both hunger and longing in satisfaction.

Hers is a life that captures the hope inside mourning and turns life into the possibility of a dance. So to my lady (God's really) I dedicate this book about following.

THE MATH OF LENT

Blessed Addition... Consider in this season 'what God might add to your life' from the sufferings of Christ. How, through you, in this season of Lent, He might add...

- ➢ an act of love, or;
- ➢ time of prayer, or;
- ➢ new friendship, or;
- ➢ new discipline of the body.

Blessed Subtraction... Or Consider 'what God might remove from your life' as you identify with Christ in his suffering. How, through you, in this season, He might remove...

- ➢ pleasure of the body, or;
- ➢ pleasure of the eye, or;
- ➢ pleasure of work.

CONTENTS

	Introduction	IV
	Understanding This Book	VI
	Dedication	IX
	The Math of Lent	X
1	THE PLACE …The Journey Home Begins	Pg 12
2	DARK PLACES, FAMILIAR PLACES …Coming to Terms with Loss	Pg #40
3	BEYOND FEAR …Recapturing Important Themes	Pg #62
4	FACING SOUTH …On the Journey to Jerusalem	Pg #96
5	COMFORT AND LOSS …The Approaching Sorrow Amid Signs of Hope	Pg #124
6	A PAUSE, BEFORE THE STORM …The Place of Jericho & Bethany, just Before	Pg #150
7	THE CUP …Will You also Drink with Me?	Pg #180
	EPILOGUE—EASTER SUNDAY	Pg #212
	Lent Rite (Entering the Story)	Pg #218
	Other Books by the Author	Pg #229
	About the Author	Pg #232

1 THE PLACE
...The Journey Home Begins

INVOCATION:

FATHER OF OUR LORD, JESUS. SOMETIMES YOU LEAD US INTO THE DEEP WATERS AND OUR LITTLE BOAT SEEMS SO SMALL. AND THEN, FATHER, YOU ALLOW THE WINDS TO GATHER FORCE TURNING THE STILL WATERS OF OUR LIVES INTO VIOLENT WAVES, TOSSING US FIRST ONE WAY AND THEN ANOTHER. WE ARE AFRAID THAT THE RISING WATERS SEEPING INTO OUR LITTLE BOAT WILL BECOME MORE THAN WE CAN MANAGE. "MASTER!" WE CRY. "WE ARE GOING TO DROWN! WAKE UP! REBUKE THE WIND, STILL THE WAVES! COME, JESUS AND CALM OUR FEARS".

AND YOU DO. THANK YOU AND FORGIVE US OUR FEAR INDUCED FAITHLESSNESS. AMEN.

ADAPTED FROM LUKE 8: 22-25

PSALM OF THE WEEK: PSALM 42

QUOTE OF THE WEEK: HEALING BEGINS WITH OUR TAKING OUR PAIN OUT OF ITS DIABOLIC ISOLATION AND SEEING THAT WHATEVER WE SUFFER, WE SUFFER IT IN COMMUNION WITH ALL OF HUMANITY, AND YES, ALL OF CREATION.

FROM "TURN MY MOURNING INTO DANCING" BY HENRI NOUWEN, PG #5,6

DAILY SCRIPTURES:

MONDAY—MATTHEW 5: 1,2 & JOHN 6: 16-58
TUESDAY—MATTHEW 5:3-9 & 16: 13-21
         & JOHN 1: 43-50
WEDNESDAY—MATTHEW 5: 13-16 & 6:1-4
         & I PETER 2: 1-12
THURSDAY—MATTHEW 2:19-23 & 5:17-20
FRIDAY—MATTHEW 5:10-12 & 16:21-28
SATURDAY—MATTHEW 6: 9-15 & MARK 9: 2-8
         & I KINGS 18:21-39
SUNDAY—MATTHEW 5:33-37 & MALACHI 4:1-5
         & MARK 9: 9-13 & JAMES 5: 7-12

Turn My Mourning Into Dancing
by Henri Nouwen
Page #11

When I came to Daybreak, the community of ministry to disabled people where I have been pastor, I was experiencing a great deal of personal pain. Many years in the world of academics, my travels among the poor in Central America, and later, my speaking around the world about what I had seen, left me deflated. My schedule kept me running hard and fast. Rather than providing an escape from my own inner conflicts, my scurrying from speaking engagement to speaking engagement only intensified my inner turmoil. And because of my schedule, I could not fully face my pain. I carried on with the illusion that I was in control, that I could avoid what I did not want to face within myself and in the world around me.

But when I arrived, I witnessed the enormous suffering of the mentally and physically handicapped persons living here. I came gradually to see my painful problems in a new light. I realized they formed part of a much larger suffering. And I found through that insight new energy to live amid my own hardship and pain.

I realized that healing begins with our taking our pain out of its diabolic isolation and seeing that whatever we suffer, we suffer it in communion with all of humanity, and yes, all of creation. In so doing, we become participants in the great battle

AGAINST THE POWERS OF DARKNESS. OUR LITTLE LIVES PARTICIPATE IN SOMETHING LARGER.

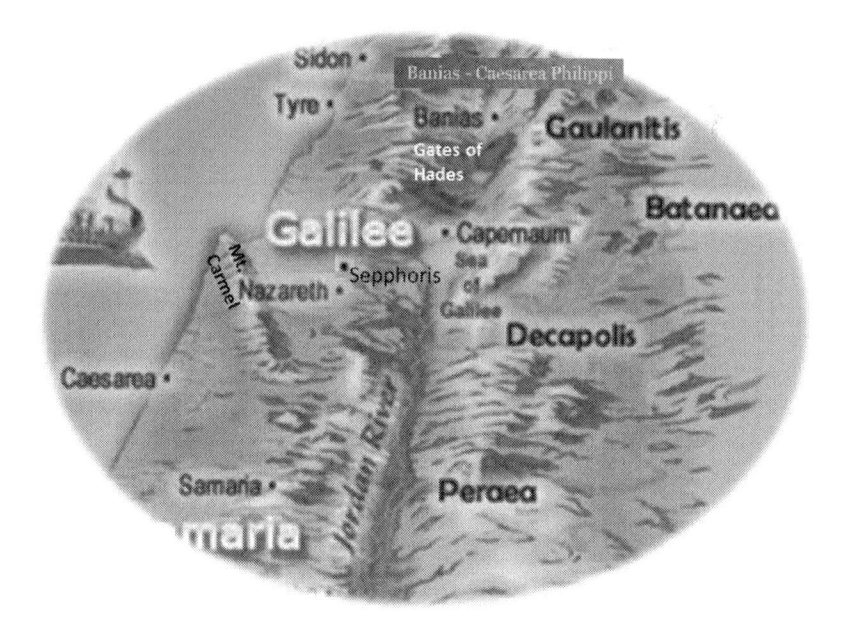

Week-1: Monday— MATTHEW 5: 1,2 & JOHN 6: 16-58

STORY 1—THE PLACE

'Why north? Why Caesarea Philippi?' John's thoughts were wandering, as, it seemed to him, his Master's steps were.

The two previous days had been dramatic. A sudden storm on Galilee, creating swells so high that even an experienced fisherman, as John was, became terrified. Just as suddenly Jesus appeared and with him the wind died. *"Who is this? Even the wind and the waves obey him!"* (Mark 4: 41). John's memory now fully awakened, remembered still more. 'Just moments before,' he reflected, 'they were lost to the sea, yet as the fog lifted, dry land appeared just off their bow. ...So why?', John's thoughts were racing, 'Why am I so troubled with him?'

The day prior Jesus had fed five thousand men, plus women and children, with nothing more than the offering of a small boy that Phillip had found. 'That's why they came! ...and Jesus rebuked them. *"I tell you the truth,"'* John could still hear the sting of his master's words. *"'You are looking for me, not because you saw miraculous signs, but because you ate the loaves and had your fill. Do not work for food that spoils, but for food that endures to eternal life'"* (John 6: 26b, 27a) John had been turning over in his mind Jesus rebuke and the children of Israel's response all day. 'Why?' he thought, 'was his master so hard on those who clearly wanted more of his life and teachings? We're not even we, his closest friends motivated by human needs?'

Looking up, John noticed Jesus out front, leading north. 'He clearly knew where he is going.' Jesus and Judas Iscariot were in a deep and intense conversation. 'Judas,' John laughed to himself, 'was always passionate, especially when he was wrong!' His thoughts betrayed his prejudices. 'Now if there were someone who needed a rebuke, it was Judas Iscariot.' For a moment the beauty of Mt. Hermon, in the distance captured his attention. But it was short lived. 'Iscariot, aptly named,' he thought. Iscariot had a double meaning and John knew both. In Hebrew it simply placed his ancestry in Kerioth, in southern Palestine. But it was a double-edged sword, for in Latin it carried the weight of history, meaning 'dagger man. And there is something about Judas, I do not trust.' John's heart felt a moment of anxious guilt and so he shook his thoughts away and the darkness of his spirit, with them.

John's focus turned to the sheer beauty of Caesarea Philippi. He, with the twelve crossed under the portico, cut out of mountain rock and entered this city where Herod the Great had built a temple, in honor of Augustus. The colonnades on both sides of the boulevard rose, as if to heaven, enlarging the doubt inside John's heart. 'Why here? Why had Jesus left the tensions surrounding his own difficult words, to come here?' Jesus words from the day before poured into John's memory, rolling like thunder. *"I tell you the truth, unless you eat the flesh of the Son of Man and drink his blood, you have no life in you. Whoever eats my flesh and drinks my blood has eternal life, and I will raise him up at the last day. For my flesh is real food and my blood is real drink"* (John 6: 53b-55). 'These were images no Jew could stomach without struggle,' John's feelings found their source, the anxiety again rising within. 'They were the words of the pagan religions surrounding Israel.' John glanced to his right and left and saw the market place filled with the images of ancient and new gods, of Pan and Rome's emperors, even now being touted as gods. His heart was torn as he looked again to Jesus, who apparently was momentarily in a casual and light hearted conversation with a shop keeper, a seller of these dead stones. 'His words about eating his flesh… they were rooted in pagan ideas, buried in the mystery religions, filled with ideas about drinking the blood of the sons of the gods. The Baptist would never!...' John shook the thought away.

John remembered Jesus question to the twelve, when most of the crowds had left, frustrated with the edge in his voice and the substance of his words. *'You do not want to leave too, do you?'* (John 6: 67). Peter's impassioned response echoed in John's heart. *'Lord, to whom shall we go? ...We believe and know that you are the Holy one of God'"* (John 6:69).

Suddenly John stopped. The other ten pushed on past him, following Judas and Jesus. In front of John and to his right was a statue, some ten feet in height, dedicated to the honor of Caesar Augustus, god of the Empire. 'Why? Why here?', John's troubled thoughts continued.

(Italics are actual quotes from texts referenced)

Reflections on "The Place"

Consider where Jesus steps have led you...

Q: Have you ever felt like John, wondering if Jesus had led you to a place where you could not go? …Were you filled with fear, guilt perhaps, or simply torn, divided within?

Week-1: TUESDAY— MATTHEW 5:3-9 & 16: 13-21
& JOHN 1: 43-50

STORY 2—THE REVELATION

"You are the Christ, the Son of the living God" (Matthew 16: 16b). John looked to his right, past Jesus and to Peter. The fire snapped as a flame burst, as if to underscore his confession.

Looking out across the small pool of water and into the shadows were the Gates of Hades. This place was the very heart of Israel's disastrous flirtation with the gods of the pagans, over centuries. This was the gate through which all gods, according to ancient myths, would descend in the dark of winter and into the under-world beneath this cavern. They would re-ascend only when called for by some pagan ritual in the spring, seeking fertility and re-birth.

'Why here?', John's question reasserted itself. He had forgotten it in the relaxation of the last two days, on Mt. Hermon. Jesus had been teaching the twelve about his Father's desire to seek the lost, everywhere and in every nation, healing the empty spaces in men and between men. At midday Jesus brought the twelve to the center of hedonism, to this very unholy place. 'Everyone,' John's heart suddenly realized the implications of this place. 'Everyone, Jew and gentile, worshipers of Yahweh and Pan and the emperor were to be included in his mission'.

"Who do you say I am?" (Matthew 16: 15b). These words suddenly crashed in upon John's thoughts, with power. 'Who do I say?' John's thoughts were interrupted as Jesus continued speaking. 'No, he was blessing Peter. *"Blessed*

are you, Simon, son of Jonah, for this was not revealed to you by man, but by my Father in heaven. And I tell you that you are Peter, and on this rock I will build my church, and the gates of Hades will not overcome it" (Matthew 16: 17b, 18).

Then Jesus went on and spoke quietly, as if to emphasize the import of his words and hide them from surrounding minions, perhaps. John listened intently. "and, it is here, in this very center of pagan life that I must build what I will call, my Church." Jesus stood and taking a branch near him walked to the fire to strike it further. "Soon, I am sending you through these gates," pointing now to the cavern before them, "and into the world to bring light, …to be light." Jesus stared for a moment into the brightness of the fire before continuing. *"I will give you the keys of the kingdom of heaven; whatever you bind on earth will be bound in heaven and whatever you loose on earth will be loosed in heaven"* (Matthew 17: 19).

Silence, deep and serene, even mystical, followed. Each of the twelve looked into the fire with Jesus, occasionally glancing up to one another, especially to Peter and John as if to gaze into their thoughts. 'That's why.' John's thoughts again turned inward. 'This is why my master brought us here.' Then Jesus interrupted the silence and warned them not to tell anyone he was the Christ.

It was here, at the Gates of Hades, that John first knew that his very Jewish world, into which he had been born, was about to change. Nathaniel's confession, almost three years earlier, echoed against the walls of John's mind, now filled with the images of this rock cavern in front of him. "Rabbi, you are the Son of God; you are the King of Israel" (John 1: 49b). 'King of Israel,' John's heart was now speaking with in. 'King of Israel… That's not why he came into the world, was it?'

(Italics are actual quotes from texts referenced)

Reflections on "The Revelation"

Q: How has your own perception of Jesus grown or changed over the years, since you first believed?

Q: Who do you say, he is? ...by your thoughts, your words or your actions?

Write out your thoughts, or turn them into a prayer.

Week-1: WEDNESDAY—MATTHEW 5: 13-16 & 6:1-4 & I PETER 2: 1-12

Story 3—Living Stones

It was good to once again be on familiar ground. The Sea of Galilee, like a crystal in the sun's light, reflected the beauty of creation. Her deep blue beckoned, especially to us who were fisherman by trade. Standing in the market place of Sepphoris near the crest of the hill we could see a panorama of the world in which six of our twelve had grown up.

To the west was Mt. Carmel, the place where Elijah had confronted the priests of Baal. My heart and mind were just now beginning to understand that Jesus mission was similar to Elijah's. Like him, we were about to usher in a new age. But instead of cleansing Israel and the nations by means of violence, we would enter into every city, every faith with the news of One whose presence and words fulfilled the longing of every human heart and culture.

Turning around to the east and gazing again upon the sea of Galilee my thoughts turned to how Jeshua's teachings related to the place upon which my feet stood. Since Caesarea Philippi and the retreat center at the Gates of Hades Jesus had been using the phrase 'Gospel', repeatedly. Gospel was a word reserved to the Emperors of Rome. It simply meant news, filled with life. Any Word from the Emperor was considered within the empire as transformational, life changing, powerful. It mattered not if the news was good or bad, pleasant or powerful. If the Emperor said it, it was a Word that made the world different.

And my Rabbi had been using that term of himself and of his words, since Peter's confession.

Standing in the center of Sepphoris, a city just five miles from Nazareth, Jesus and Mary's village and not ten miles from my home in Bethsaida, I began to realize that our little world, indeed the whole world was about to change. Jeshua, of Nazareth, was the Gospel, bringing a life altering Word into a new age. 'Sepphoris', the administrative capital of Herod Antipas, Tetrarch of Galilee and Peraea, I realized 'could one day be a ghost town, but Nazareth's son would live forever.'

Jeshua was now directing us down the hill toward the beautiful theatre nestled against the back side of the hill upon which we now stood. A month of Sabbaths before and I would have wondered why Jeshua was taking us to such a pagan and vulgar place.

Herod Antipas had poured money into this city and theatre in honor of himself. Jesus knew this place well for he had worked with his papa, helping in its construction. As we made our way down the wide streets with their majestic columns rising toward the sun I pointed out to the others the tablets of stone that Jeshua's papa had carved into the base of each column. Earlier that day Jesus had confided in me that his papa had been employed by Herod's administrator, Cuza, to create something culturally acceptable to the Jews who would visit and do business in this city. And so Joseph had created stone tablets, one on each column with picturesque carvings from the Hebrew Story formed into the base of the column.

Gathering us near one of columns, just outside the theatre, Jesus restated one of the thematic messages of his mission. *"You are the light of the world. A town built on a hill cannot be hidden. Neither do people light a lamp and put it under a bowl. Instead they put in on its stand, and it gives light to everyone in the house. In the same way, let your light shine before men, that they may see your good deeds and glorify your Father in heaven"* (Matthew 5: 14-16). Jesus had begun walking again as he spoke, the context radically filling his familiar teaching with new meaning. He continued, "I want you to be living stones, in a great city. You are to become the foundational life of the city with the very breath of Yahweh filling each word you speak. And then, looking up, a smile spreading across his face and eyes, he prayed. "Holy Father, may these whom You have given me become living pillars in Your world, pointing the way, Father, to Your beautiful city."

My own heart was deeply moved. 'How could I have questioned Jesus mission or allowed my spirit to become anxious over his words and actions as I had at Caesarea?' I felt ashamed.

Quietly, Jesus turned and moved further down the street and entered under the portico opening to the theatre. He walked into a place no Jew, let alone a Rabbi would dare enter for entertainment and took a seat. 'What were we to do?' We followed.

Once again Jesus placed his familiar teachings in a new and scandalous context with the meaning exploding in our hearts. "Be careful," he began, "not to do your 'acts of righteousness before men, to be seen by them. *If you do, you will have no reward from your Father in heaven. So when you give to the needy, do not announce it with trumpets, as the hypocrites do in the synagogues and on the streets, to be honored by men.* (Matthew 6:1-2a). 'Trumpets, hypocrites (actors)...' My mind rushed to absorb the layered meanings. All of us Jews were familiar with the huge and golden trumpets in the Holy Temple in Jerusalem. They were the vessels for giving offerings to Yahweh. The righteous would approach and pour out their coins in the narrow top of the trumpet, obviously proud that their generous gift would noisily crash down the narrow opening, clanging against the metal sides until finding their home with a thud at the bottom of this huge vessel.

Just then, from behind us, a trumpet blew at the top of the amphitheater, above the seating. With each trumpet an actor (hypocrite as we knew them to be) would enter, music interweaving the dramatic presentation to give added meaning, filling our senses with sight and sound. We turned away from listening to Jesus for a moment to watch the actors (hypocrites) practice. None of us, except Jeshua, had ever seen a play. We gathered in closer, entranced by the powerful images unfolding. 'Actors playing, trumpets announcing.' My thoughts suddenly turned inward. 'How much of my own religious fervor with the Baptist and now with Jeshua had been simply that of an actor playing, a trumpet sounding?'

Only after the actors finished practicing did we leave, again following Jesus, but in silence. We knew where we were headed. To Cuza's home, where Joanna, his wife, would see that we received an awesome meal and a bath and our own bed. Joanna had been supporting Jesus mission from the beginning.

As I walked past one of the colonnades I stopped, noticing again the Hebrew carvings in its base. On it—just under a carving of what appeared to be the tent of meeting in the desert, a great cloud gathering above—and in Hebrew, were the Words of the prophet Moses. "And he passed in front of Moses, proclaiming, 'The LORD, the LORD, the compassionate and gracious God, slow to anger, abounding in love and faithfulness, maintaining love to thousands, and forgiving wickedness, rebellion and sin'" (Exodus 34: 6,7a). 'You are the light of the world', Jesus had said. "Papa," I breathed a silent prayer, using Jeshua's own invocation for the first time. "Forgive me for acting and judging, for fear of men's acceptance. Help me to live as a light. Allow me to become a living stone, a pillar rising in the most pagan place you choose, trumpeting only Your love and mercy! Amen."

My prayer was interrupted as I felt a hand, Jeshua's hand gently lay on my shoulder. The other eleven were at some distance up the hill, toward the center of the city. Jeshua and I were alone. I turned to him, trickles of water having formed in my eyes and dropping to my cheeks. He embraced me.

How I loved him in that moment. "Forgive me, Master," was all I could say.

Reflections on "Living Stones"

Consider the light of Christ in you, your family and church:

Q: Does it shine brightly? ...Why? ...Why not?

Q: Are you a living stone of God, foundational to the health of your city? ...How so? ...Why not?

Write out your thoughts, or turn it to a prayer:

Week-1: THURSDAY-- MATTHEW 2:19-23 & 5:17-20
STORY 4—REFLECTIONS

Jesus was standing, leaning really, against the entrance to his papa's workspace, with one hand resting above him as if holding the portico up, his face cuddled up against his extended arm. He seemed to melt into the wood framed entrance, silent, deep in memories.

I approached him slowly, silently so that I would not disturb his thoughts. I took up a position opposite his, just in front, my hands resting behind me like a kind of pillow as I leaned against the portico wall. Some time passed as we stood, silently looking into an open courtyard of what appeared to be a mason's shop, now abandoned.

Mary, Jeshua's mother, was on the other side of this open space in her cooking area, busy preparing the evening meal for her son and the twelve and whoever might drop in to say hi to Mary's rather famous rabbi.

"I miss him." I knew that Jeshua must be speaking of his papa, my uncle. "As do I," I responded some seconds later. Jeshua continued, now turning toward me and allowing his body to slide down the rock wall just beyond the wood frame. I remained absolutely still, knowing I was hearing his inmost thoughts. "I remember papa teaching the students of the village, as he worked with his hands. Such skill." Looking deep into my eyes, his moist, he continued. "It was here that he formed all the stone foundations for Sepphoris." Yesterday's visit to Sepphoris was still vivid. I inserted, "The carvings of Israel." My cousin nodded. "When papa's hands moved over stone, cutting, carving and shaping it was a pleasure just to watch. His eyes were alive with joy. But it was his words that carved into my heart." Jeshua looked to his right and deeper into the work area. "Papa spoke of Moses law as though it were living." Then Jeshua's voice deepened as if to mimic his papa. "The law is not made for stone, as you see here, but for the human heart. Yahweh desires to write his law into your heart so that God's goodness beats within…" Jeshua lay his head back to rest against the rock wall. "Then papa would hammer and grunt as he shaped the stone into the image in his own heart. Only then would he pick up the tablet and finish his teaching." Again, in a voice larger than his own, Jeshua remembered his papa's words. "Yahweh desires that you and I become living stones." Jeshua smiled. "Then his eyes would pierce into one of us children as he spoke. 'You are a work of art, a sign pointing toward God!'" Jeshua laughed. "Then papa would laugh… class dismissed." Jeshua said nothing for a few moments and then looking over to me, added. "John, I miss him."

Reflections on "Reflections"

Consider the purpose of God's law.

Q: Is God's law (truth) alive in you?

Q: Do you live it in such a way as to be inviting to those you mentor or whose life you touch?

Q: To whom are The Book?

Pray for them and for yourself as a living book of God:

Week-1: FRIDAY— MATTHEW 5:10-12 & 16:21-28

STORY 5—PREMONITIONS

It had been about a week now. Our spirits were a little more relaxed, in Mary's presence. Nazareth was a simple, beautiful village. The smells, sights and sounds gave all of us a sense of the familiar, of family; of what we had each left to follow the Master.

Jesus though, seemed at a distance. His eyes often looked through us, as if to something beyond. His usual light hearted laughter was absent. A darkened mood surrounded him.

I was seated in the courtyard when I felt his hand touch my shoulders. Peter and James were with him. He motioned me to follow. We made our way down the hillside from Nazareth to the cross road. From there we could go to the Sea or Sepphoris or Jericho. Jesus began walking up into the hill country between Nazareth and Jericho, but turning toward the west.

Most of the day, Jesus was walking on ahead of us, alone, perhaps in prayer. Peter, James and I were bantering with each other, feeling pretty good about ourselves. After all, we were the first among our brothers. 'When the Master came into his kingdom', I allowed myself a smile, 'two of us would surely be on his left and his right.'

Jesus led us higher into the hill country. The view was incredible. Far in the west was Mt. Carmel, the place where Elijah had confronted the priests of the Baals. The valley before us was the place where the prophet Ezekiel saw a great battle coming at the end of time, the time of the Messiah.

That evening, as dusk approached, we made camp. It was not long before the sounds of a crackling fire mingled with view of Megiddo before us. Jesus came closer to us and spoke his first words since we had left Nazareth. He shared in some detail his wilderness journey, following his baptism some three years previous. Of the three, only I had witnessed Jeshua's baptism. My mind returned to the Baptist, may his memory be ever blessed, and to his words. 'I hear you Papa,' he had said, 'This is my beloved Son, with whom I am pleased.' And at that moment a beautiful white dove swooped down from the heavens where he had been circling and came to light of Jeshua's shoulder. Suddenly the fire snapped, helping me to return to this moment and the story Jeshua was telling.

As Jeshua stared into the valley below, his voice shifted, as one does when he no longer is telling a story, but living it. *"'All this I will give you,'* Lucifer continued, *'if you will bow down and worship me'"* (Matthew 4:9). Jeshua paused.

To this day I do not know what it was that I saw, if in fact I really perceived anything real. It was more like a shadowy presence. Before me, in the valley below, were gathered armies from a multitude of nations.

I did not recognize any of their banners. They were not Roman. Their armaments were unlike any I had seen in my time. Some appeared to be large insects, perhaps locusts, though the armaments were not living, but made of some kind of armor. Others looked more like huge behemoths, with piercing swords out front. Suddenly Jeshua brought me back to the mountain as he cried out. *"Away from me Satan! For it is written: worship the LORD your God, and serve him only"* (Matthew 4: 10b). His face was filled with terror I had never seen. Drops of sweat poured down upon him. We all stood motionless, afraid to speak, until, Peter, bless his heart. He stepped forward toward Jesus and spoke with passion. Peter seemed oblivious to the fact that Jeshua seemed not to be listening, at least not to him.

"Master," Peter began. "At Hermon you spoke of being rejected in Jerusalem by the Chief Priests and the elders of Israel." Peter stepped closer still and spoke directly into the Master's face. Jeshua continued to just stare into the night, for dusk had now settled into a shadowy darkness.

"Master!" Peter was now emphatic. "It must not come to that! The Chief Priests and elders must be made to recognize who you are!" Jeshua's head turned slightly so that he was now looking directly into my cousin's eyes. To his credit, Peter shut up. Jeshua spoke firmly, but with a deep sadness. *"Get behind me, Satan! You are a stumbling block to me; you do not have in mind the things of God, but the things of men"* (Matthew 16: 23b). With that Jesus turned and walked alone higher up into the mountain.

Slowly, Peter turned back to James and me. You could see the complete betrayal that he felt. After some moments, James broke the silence. "Come, brother, come cousin," he spoke gently while turning to face the fire. "Let's eat."

Reflections on "Premonitions"

Imagine the cost to Jesus in the weeks approaching Jerusalem.

Q: How do you handle difficult spaces in your journey in life? What do you do? ...Run, hide, strike out in anger, spend money, stay busy, sleep, eat, pray, listen?

Reflect and pray:

> *"I am less likely to deny my suffering when I learn how God uses it to mold me and draw me closer to him. I will be less likely to see my pains as interruptions to my plans and more able to see them*

as the means for God to make me ready to receive him. I let Christ live near my hurts and distractions."
Henri Nouwen in "Turn My Mourning Into Dancing", pg #11

Week-1: SATURDAY— MATTHEW 6: 9-15 & MARK 9: 2-8
& I KINGS 18:21-39

STORY 6—VISIONS

Peter woke first. When fully awake, he reached over with his hands to shake me and my brother James awake. Slowly I emerged from a deep rest, as one does coming out of a thick fog into a clear sun filled day. I did not wish to wake up. I had fallen asleep thinking of Mt. Carmel in the distance and of Elijah's fearless challenge to the people before the four hundred priests of Baal. *"How long will you waver between two opinions? If the LORD is God, follow him; but if Baal is God, follow him,"* he had asked (I Kings 18: 21b). The fire had fallen from the heavens consuming the sacrifice, leaving only a steamy mist where once water had been. In my sleep, I had entered into the crowd as one of them. We fell as one to the ground, misty clouds rising from the fiery demonstration of God's power. We were all crying out... *"The LORD—he is God! The LORD—he is God!"* (I Kings 18: 39b).

"John!" I heard my name and in my dream state it felt as though the ground were shaking. "John, wake up!" I heard it again and again, the voice slowly pulling me away from my dream and into another moment no less intense. As the dream faded, filled as it was with fire and smoke and a mysterious rising cloud of steam, I became aware of another cloud just in front of Peter and James, both fixated upon it.

Inside were colors of the rainbow, swirling as if in a dance. From within the cloud appeared a man for whom the layered colors were dancing, gently caressing him, each touch a release of light. The reds, greens, yellows and blues were slowly coming to rest at his feet creating a single color of brilliant white light, which came to envelop him like clothes made of silk. I fell to my knees, as I had in my dream. Peter and James were already prostrate before the unfolding vision. I heard myself whispering again the words echoing from Mt. Carmel… *"The LORD—he is God! The LORD—he is God!"* (I Kings 18: 39b). I had the distinct sense that a great host were surrounding us, repeating the same words, though I could not hear or see them.

As my eyes adjusted to the dazzling light, I looked up and could make out the face of the one before me. It was my Master and Rabbi, Jeshua! I could now see into the cloud well enough to see two others, one to the right of Jeshua and one to the left. I do not know how I knew, but my spirit recognized one as Moses, the other as Elijah. It was the same Elijah as in my dream.

I trembled with fear, aware that my soul was shaking within. I could feel my heart racing. Next, I heard my cousin, Peter, crying out. "Rabbi!" Apparently, he also recognized Jeshua. "Rabbi!", he again exclaimed, *"it is good for us to be here. Let us put up three shelters—one for you, one for Moses and one for Elijah"* (Mark 9:5). His idea, it seemed, was an appropriate response. Seized with fear, at least talking helped.

Suddenly, as if in response to Peter's suggestion, another cloud, filled with white lightening came from the heavens, enveloping Jeshua, Moses and Elijah and removing them from our sight. From within this second cloud a voice thundered. *"This is my Son, whom I love. Listen to him!"* (Mark 9:7c). At the sound of this voice I again fell prostrate to the ground and buried my face in absolute terror.

An eerie silence followed, around and within. There was no wind or signs of life; no birds singing or trees rustling. After what seemed minutes I felt his touch and heard his voice, soft, even playful. "John, Peter, James, sit up and follow." We did.

Reflections on "Visions"

Q: Have you ever felt a moment of absolute terror before God? ...or, perhaps, Awe? ...or mystery?

Describe it or write a prayer in quest of this God who is 'other' as well as 'near':

Week-1: SUNDAY— MATTHEW 5:33-37 & MALACHI 4:1-5 & MARK 9: 9-13 & JAMES 5: 7-12

MY THOUGHTS 1—WHEN VISIONS CEASE

Coming down from the Mount of Transfiguration, Jesus warned the three not to tell anyone. Why?

The reason becomes clear in light of their conversation. They asked Jesus, *"Why do the teachers of the law say that Elijah must come first?"* (Mark 9: 11b). This question follows their discussion of Jesus promised resurrection. ...And why resurrection? Because, now, they were ready to begin facing, even a little, the recent and dark confessions of their master about his approaching rejection, suffering and death.

Resurrection always follows death and loss. This profound moment with Jesus, Elijah and Moses and the thundering voice of God in the heavens gave them the confidence they needed to begin facing the demands of the weeks ahead.

It was the understanding of the Rabbis of the time that when the end came with its resurrection and judgment, Elijah would be present once again. Had not Malachi promised, *"Surely the day is coming; it will burn like a furnace... See, I will send you the prophet Elijah before the great and dreadful day of the LORD comes. He will turn the hearts of the parents to their children, and the hearts of the children to their parents..."* (Malachi 4:1a, 5, 6a).

So, in light of the clear revelation from heaven—not Peters only—that Jesus was the very Son of the living God, they were really asking, 'Where's Elijah?' Put differently, they were asking Jesus to help reconcile his approaching suffering with God's promise that a new day of reconciliation and renewal would come in the Messiah and his prophet.

Jesus response is interesting. To the first question, 'Where's Elijah?', Jesus affirmed that he has come in the presence of the Baptist. And his preaching did bring to Israel renewal and reconciliation by way of repentance and water. But to the second question, 'what is the place of suffering inside God's new age?', Jesus simply reminded them that John also suffered. John also was required to give his life in order that this new age lives.

By example, Jesus is addressing their eschatology, their understanding of 'the glorious new age' by revealing the 'way of suffering'. It is as though he said, 'I have come and with me all the glory of the Father has come. But I have come to bring glory by way of suffering!'

Reflections on "When Visions Cease"

Consider the times in which you live.

Q: Is there room in your own understanding of salvation to include suffering as redemptive? ...your own and those of every human and animal and plant around you?

Again, consider Nouwen:

> "An early step in the dance sounds very simple, though often will not come easily: We are called to grieve our losses. It seems paradoxical, but healing and dancing begin with looking squarely at what causes us pain. We face the secret losses that have paralyzed us and kept us imprisoned in denial or shame or guilt. We do not nurse the illusion that we can hopscotch our way through difficulties. For by trying to hide parts of our story from God's eye and

our own consciousness, we become judges of our own past. We limit divine mercy to our human fears. Our efforts to disconnect ourselves from our own suffering end up disconnecting our suffering from God's suffering for us. The way out of our loss and hurt is in and through. When Jesus said, "for I have come to call not the righteous but sinners" (Matt. 9:13), *he affirmed that only those who can face their wounded condition can be available for healing and enter a new way of living.*
Sometimes we need to ask ourselves just what our losses are..."
Henri Nouwen, in "Turn My Mourning Into Dancing", page 6, 7

Q: So why does God allow injustice to remain, even flourish?

Your Thoughts? Turn them to listening for the voice of God…

Who Am I?

2 Dark Places, Familiar Places
...Coming to Terms with Loss

INVOCATION:

Save me, O God, for the waters have come up to my neck. I sink in the miry depths, where there is no foothold. I have come into the deep waters; the floods engulf me. I am worn out calling for help; my throat is parched. My eyes fail, looking for my God...

O Father of all spirits, I take comfort in knowing that my prayer was David's prayer when in trouble and that David's prayer was Your Son's prayer as Golgotha approached.

Answer me, O Lord, out of the goodness of your love; in your great mercy turn to me. I am never completely alone. Thank you, Father. Amen.

-*Italics from Psalm 69: 1-3, 16*

PSALM OF THE WEEK: Psalm 69

Who Am I?

QUOTE OF THE WEEK: ONE OF LIFE'S GREAT QUESTIONS CENTERS NOT ON WHAT HAPPENS TO US, BUT RATHER, HOW WE WILL LIVE IN AND THROUGH WHATEVER HAPPENS.

FROM "TURN MY MOURNING INTO DANCING" BY HENRI NOUWEN, PG #12

DAILY SCRIPTURES:

MONDAY—MATTHEW 6: 5-8 & MARK 9: 30-32

TUESDAY—MATTHEW 6:9-15 & HEBREWS 4: 14-16

WEDNESDAY—MATTHEW 6:16-18 & MARK 9:14-27

THURSDAY—MATTHEW 5:21-26 & MARK 9: 30, 38-41

FRIDAY—JOHN 15: 1-12 & MATTHEW 18: 1-5

SATURDAY—MATTHEW 7:7-12 & MARK 9:28-30

SUNDAY—MATTHEW 5:3 & 6:25-27 & 8:14-17 & II CORINTHIANS 11:24-30 & 12:7-10

JOINING IN THE LARGER DANCE
From
Turn My Mourning Into Dancing
by Henri Nouwen
Page #13, 14

Mourning makes us poor; it powerfully reminds us of our smallness. But it is precisely here, in that pain or poverty or awkwardness, that the Dancer invites us to rise up and take the first steps. For in our suffering, not apart from it, Jesus enters our sadness, takes us by the hand, pulls us gently up to stand, and invites us to dance. We find the way to pray, as the psalmist did, "You have turned my mourning into dancing" (Ps. 30:11), because at the center of our grief we find the grace of God. And as we dance, we realize that we don't have to stay on the little spot of our grief, but can step beyond it. We stop centering our lives on ourselves. We pull others along with us and invite them into the larger dance. We learn to make room for others—and the Gracious Other in our midst. And when we become present to God and God's people, we find our lives richer. We come to know that all the world is our dance floor. Our step grows lighter because God has called out others to dance as well.

Week-2: MONDAY—MATTHEW 6: 5-8 & MARK 9: 30-32
STORY 7—ALONE

Coming down from the mountain, we again came to the main road. Jesus turned north towards Nazareth and the Sea. Jesus had said nothing more to us since our brief conversation about Elijah while descending from the Mount of his appearing. With each step away from Elijah and Moses, Jeshua's mood seemed to darken. James, Peter and I allowed the Master at some distance.

That evening we made camp along the road. Jesus had taken a turn off the road that brought us below Nazareth and toward the Sea, not far Capernaum, and just beyond and around the sea was Bethsaida, my home town. The smell of the Sea of Galilee captured me suddenly, flooding my spirit with a familiar peace. I missed home and family, friends, my mama and papa.

As dusk turned to darkness and the last sun light touched the eastern shore of Galilee, Jesus looked up, from his prayers. We were all gathered around the fire, which was crackling and casting the first shadows of the evening on the trees surrounding us. Jesus voice was soft, intense. *"The son of man,"* he began slowly, *"is going to be delivered into the hands of men. They will kill him, and after three days he will rise"* (Mark 9:31).

I looked into his eyes, soft, yet dark. He was looking intently into the fire as if for comfort. I sat in complete silence, turning my eyes to the fire as well. I was afraid to respond. 'How', I wondered, 'can this be? Surely the Voice from heaven, the

One who spoke within the lightening would come to the defense of my master.'

Looking back on that moment, many years removed, I came to realize that Jeshua was not simply teaching, but pleading out of his lonely burden… He was really crying out softly, "Hear me… you who are closest to me. I do not wish to be alone."

But we did not hear. We simply stared with Jesus into the fire. One by one we took our leave in silence, pulling our tunics around us and lay down to sleep. The previous day had left us all exhausted. We all fell asleep. All but Jesus. He was alone.

Reflections on "Alone"

Q: Have you ever known such a lonely place in your life? …How did this moment impact your faith, your relationships, your confidence?

Terry is suggesting that Jesus lived fully inside the loss that approached, feeling it's sadness and stress, experiencing its loneliness.

Q: How does such a view of Jesus strike you? …What are the implications?

Write out a prayer to God or a reflection from God to you:

Week-2: TUESDAY—Matthew 6:9-15 & Hebrews 4: 14-16
My Thoughts 2—Aloneness and Loneliness

I love nothing more than being alone, thinking, feeling, writing, reading; especially when I'm in a spacious place in the mountains or desert or, even, alone in a crowd at a fine restaurant, being served. Why? Because I enjoy and trust me and God. These creative reflections, even internal humor that evoke a smile sometimes within the quiet of my thoughts or in the inter-relation of God thoughts—those emotive filled impressions that have the signature of God in them and feel and sound like Jesus's voice.

I hate feeling lonely. In this space it matters not where I am or who I am with. It is a sense of being 'out of fellowship' or ignored in a social connection. Those feelings can emerge in a football stadium of thousands or as I walk Alki beach in Seattle. Always, ever it is a sense of being lost to another or God or to my own best self. It is a lonely place.

And so, in the last weeks of Jesus there is a hint of such moments we saw earlier and will see again; such as the Garden of Gethsemane when Jesus needs to be understood or with someone who understands—who in a silence words cannot convey communicates understanding. In his purposeful movements toward Jerusalem, loneliness is present; as is 'aloneness'.

Reflections on "Aloneness and Loneliness"

Silence shared is a powerful gift, especially in a lonely and painful place. Silence that is a wall of fear or unconcern can be just as powerfully damning.

Consider the silence in the last story told by John the apostle as Jesus is pictured reaching out in sorrow and is met instead with silent stares verses the kind of silence shared between two friends or with God, when words will not suffice and presence is enough.

Q: Do you have a friend with whom you can share silence?

Q: Have you ever entered into the gift of shared silence with God? ...How so? ...Why not?

Week-2: WEDNESDAY— Matthew 6:16-18 & Mark 9:14-27

Story 8—The Loneliness of Apparent Failure

Bethsaida is a small village nestled between the hill country and the great sea, Galilee. Our Rabbi, now very old, was wise and loving. He kept in close touch with the scribes of the Holy Temple in Jerusalem and taught well the questions inside Israel's experience and heart. Our knowledge of Elijah and his place at the end of time was the result of his teachings. From boyhood our Rabbi had taken me on as his student, preparing me for a place of leadership in the Synagogue at Capernaum. My interest in the Baptist and now Jeshua reflected his teachings.

As we approached our little village my mind was in quiet reflection. I could hear my little rabbi's voice in my heart. 'Water, living, bubbling has always been a sign of Yahweh's life. The law of Moses is to become a fresh new stream of life within you. We baptize those who are pagan in living water as a sign of Yahweh's cleansing Word bringing hope and promise to those born outside of Israel's covenant with God.' I smiled at the memory.

Today's walk was less intense, more casual than yesterday's. For one thing we were apparently going home. We were on the road to Bethsaida, having passed by Capernaum, rounding the northern shores of Galilee. Even Jeshua seemed more relaxed. He walked with us, bantering freely...until we arrived just outside our village.

A crowd of about a hundred had gathered along the sea shore. They were huddled together, facing into the center of their gathering, listening intently. James, Peter and I were able to enter into the outside of their gathering without being noticed. Not at first, anyway. Jeshua held back at a small distance. An argument of some intensity was under way. I quickly recognized the voice of Benjamin, my Rabbi, speaking with authority, challenging someone. "On whose authority have you come to Bethsaida? I hear the stories, my friends, of Jeshua. Many are good. Stories of healing and teachings of Moses being renewed, of John's Baptism in water for even the sons of Israel. All this appears of God. But Andrew..." I moved to the right and gently placed my hands on two men's shoulders to get a better view. They did not turn, so deep was their focus. Rabbi Benjamin was speaking directly to my cousin, Andrew, Peter's brother. Glancing around, I saw Judas and Bartholomew as well. Jeshua must have directed the other nine to Bethesda to meet up with us following our two-day trip into the hill country. "Andrew," my Rabbi seemed to be pleading now, "this papa and his son have suffered enough. Why have you filled Malichi," referring to the papa, "with a hope that you had not the authority or power to give?"

I stepped between the two men in front of me, opening a hole in the crowd. Peter and James followed. Rabbi Benjamin turned away from Andrew and looked in my direction. Behind me another yelled out. "Jeshua! Jeshua of Nazareth is here!" With the announcement the crowd turned their attention and seemed to move toward Jesus, as one. My rabbi came up to me in greeting, giving me a bear hug and slaps on the back. "John, son of thunder," he said, "it is always good to see you. I had heard you were now following this itinerate rabbi, as you did the Baptist, before him." I smiled. Rabbi Benjamin then moved past me with the crowd and placed himself alongside Malachi, as a good shepherd does, protecting his sheep.

Jeshua spoke first. His spirit seemed slightly agitated. "Andrew," he directed his question while looking directly at my former mentor and rabbi. *"What are you arguing with them about?"* Before Andrew could defend himself, Malachi spoke up. *"Teacher, I brought* to your disciples *my son, who*

Who Am I?

is possessed by a spirit that has robbed him of speech. Whenever it seizes him, it throws him to the ground. He foams at the mouth, gnashes his teeth and becomes rigid. I asked your disciples to drive out the spirit, but they could not."

Looking directly at Andrew and around toward Matthew, Judas and Bartholomew, Jeshua continued. *"O unbelieving generation...,"* Jeshua reached out and touched Andrew's shoulder to soften the rebuke, *"how long shall I stay with you?"* Now Jeshua smiled. *"How long shall I put up with you?"* Turning now to Malachi. *"Bring the boy to me."*

Malachi stepped forward with his son, Jacob, who looked deeply frightened, trembling slightly. Jesus asked the boy's father, *"How long has he been like this?"* With a tenderness of spirit, Jeshua reached out and touched Jacob's head, as Malachi responded. *"From childhood,"* he answered. *"It has often thrown him into fire or water to kill him. But if you can do anything, take pity on us and help us." "If you can? said Jesus,"* and looking directly at Malachi, *"everything is possible for him who believes."* Immediately Malachi exclaimed, *"I do believe; help me overcome my unbelief!"* I glanced at my friend and Rabbi, Benjamin, and noticed that he was watching intently, fully aware that another shepherd's heart was among us.

Jeshua looked up and noticed that still others were running up from the village to see the spectacle and turned his focus to Jacob, the mute. I quickly picked up the need to pre-empt the growing crowd and protect this boy. Instinctively Peter, James, Andrew and I moved to order the crowd back to give Jesus, Malachi, Jacob and Rabbi Benjamin room.

Jeshua, seeing our correction, focused his full attention to Jacob. *"You deaf and mute spirit,"* he said, *"I command you, come out of him and never enter him again."* The spirit shrieked, convulsed him violently and came out. Jacob dropped to the ground, all life appeared to be gone. Someone in the crowd before me exclaimed. "He's dead!" I turned around. Jesus simply reached over and took Jacob's hand. Jacob's eyes opened with a clarity and peace that reminded me of the pool just in front of the Gates of Hades.

While Malachi hugged his son, I turned back to my Rabbi and introduced him to Jeshua, my Master. Jeshua reached out his hand in a warm greeting and simply said, "Good shepherd, see that Malachi brings Jacob to you, as commanded by Moses for review and confirmation of his healing." With that Jesus turned to leave with the twelve following. We continued to make our way through Galilee, turning up into the hill country above Capernaum. Jesus wanted to be alone to pray and review with us the day's events.

(note: Italics are quotations from verses in Mark 9: 14-27)

Reflections on "The Loneliness of Apparent Failure"

Consider the relation between believing and miracles:

Q: Is it a mathematical equation? 100% belief = miracle done? …if not, then what is the relation?

Q: What role does time and wounds and spiritual renewal play in miraculous moments?

Write a prayer out to God for someone who has been wounded or who struggles with a life threatening or debilitating disease and keep their name before God during this season of Lent.

Week-2: THURSDAY—Matthew 5:21-26 & Mark 9: 30, 38-41
Story 9—Conflicting Emotions

We had been walking most of the morning. At first I thought Jesus was leading us back to Mt. Hermon, to the north, where the last week's events began. The darkness of Jesus prophecy concerning his suffering still hung in the air like the hot, wet heat of a summer day, following rain. Mostly it was Jesus who felt it. Andrew approached me as we walked. "When, cousin," he began, "will you tell us what happened in the hill country to the south of Nazareth. Peter won't speak of it." We, Andrew and I stopped for a moment. The others continued. "Andrew, I began…," hesitating, searching for words. "I can't." Andrew just looked at me, his eyes reflecting a kind of betrayal.

It was apparent, now, that we were not moving to the north, but further west around the sea and then up into the hills above Capernaum, toward Chorazin. Jesus found a stream, often dry in mid-summer, and moved up into the hill country to make camp, I assumed. Questions from the previous two days were swirling in my heart. 'Why were we, Peter, James, and I allowed to see into heaven and not the others? And what was the purpose?' We came from that incredible moment and into the depth of Jeshua's anguish, that first night around the fire and then the miracle, or lack of miracle for Malachi? 'About what or of whom was Jeshua initially agitated? "…Perverse generation," he had said.'

My thoughts were interrupted by the banter of the others, with whom Andrew and I had caught up. "So tell me," Bartholomew began, "that is if your majesties can divulge any secrets of the inner circle…" His laughter and sarcasm masked an apparent wound. I felt defensive. I was grateful Jeshua was walking a little ahead, apparently in prayer or deep thought. "Yes," Judas now picked up the banter. "Peter," he continued, "perhaps you were planning a strategy for the surrender of Jerusalem!" We all laughed. I was grateful the dialogue seemed to move away from us, to the coming kingdom. It did not last. Andrew piped in. "And how are you going to work out who sits on his left and right?" He was laughing. "Last time I checked, three does not go into two, well." I was shocked. Of all Jesus followers not given to jealousy, it was my cousin and deep friend who had been on this quest with me, since the days of the Baptist. Peter stopped and turned. Everyone, except the Master, stopped with him. "Look," he said. "We didn't seek Jeshua out for this honor." I thought to myself. 'Peter, poor choice of words.' But, then, that was Peter. I smiled, part of me glad he had said it. "Jeshua chose us and asked us not to let anyone know of the appearing!" "Peter!" James broke in. Peter looked over at me, knowing he had said too much. He turned, barking out orders. "Just, shut up! We're only doing what the Master asked!" With that Peter moved forward, walking alone, about half way between Jeshua and the rest of us. We all walked in silence, until the next joke.

Reflections on "Conflicting Emotions"

Q: What is your personal response to conflict? …at home? …at work? …in the Church?

This theme of 'who is in?' and 'who is out' will occupy a great deal of the attention of the twelve, even to their last evening together with Jesus.

Q: Do you see this struggle for place and acceptance in you? …in your Church?

Q: Why didn't Jesus just shut it down?

Q: What human need lies behind these kinds of conflict?

Turn to prayer your own needs or that of your family or work or church… where you see conflicted emotions about place in community?

Week-2: Friday—John 15: 1-12 & Matthew 18: 1-5

My Thoughts 3—On The Role of Conflict

my thoughts

I always perceived conflict, whether in my home or in my church, as bad. In the first years of my pastorate, I spent a lot of time avoiding it, thinking I was protecting Jesus, from the worst in us.

In my own experience in the church, whenever a pastor enters into conflict, something gives. Depending on the personality of the pastor, it is usually lay people who move on or pastors who move on. The really exceptional pastors stay and get ulcers.

God has led me to a community of faith that is diverse economically and culturally. About twenty percent of our congregation comes from the streets. We are filled with Samoan, Filipino and native American cultures. We are roughly 50% Republican and 50% Democrat. I remember welcoming a person one Sunday who was afraid to come in. He pulled me aside and confessed to an emotional illness, bi-polar. He wanted my permission to enter. I just laughed and said, "trust me, you're not alone. Come!"

Conflict is a given in our church. At one point I counted three persons on our leadership team with varying degrees of psychologically driven propensity to conflict. Usually it is good natured. Not always. Over time many have left, most have returned. I have learned that conflict is an important part of the journey. One of its benefits, when people work through it, is the sheer joy of valuing people over ideas, convictions, beliefs (political and social) and cultural differences. In the rhythms of life conflict and joy are two sides of the same coin; both valuable to community formation.

Conflict is one-way God forms our hearts; Our sanctification (conformity to God's loving purposes) is molded within conflict, if allowed to exist and in a context when fighting remains fair. The honesty with which we deal with each other is uncomfortable, at times. But so is the silence of never expressing your feelings, as is often the case, in His church.

And, yes, I struggle with ulcers.

Reflections on "The Role of Conflict"

Q: Do you enjoy any deep relations that do not include conflict?

Terry suggests that the richness, joy, texture of a Church's life is dependent, in part, on fighting fair; allowing conflict room to find real resolution.

Q: Your thoughts? ...Is this idea of 'conflict' as sanctifying (holy-love making) new to you?

Q: What do you think 'fighting fair' looks like?

Q: Is it really necessary for people to leave, when in conflict? ...When they do, should we always try to keep the door open to return? ...Even, especially, when those who leave, do so with an attitude?

Turn your thoughts and observations to prayer for your church and its journey toward great joy.

Week-2: SATURDAY—MATTHEW 7:7-12 & MARK 9:28-30
STORY 10—FAITH UNPACKED

One of my favorite moments with Jeshua and the twelve is when we are alone and able to unpack the day's events, the questions, the failures. I was still reeling from our experience in my home town, Bethsaida, the day before. Malachi had invited us to his home for a meal. Following, we had stayed with my parents for the evening. Andrew, I think it was, had asked Jeshua, "Why couldn't we drive out the demon inside Malachi's son?" Jeshua had responded simply that *"this kind can only come by prayer"* (Mark 9:28b). It was late and our discussion ended.

But now, after darkness settled in like the warm blanket a mother gives her son at bed time, Jeshua seemed to want to return to issues of faith. My heart was open. I listened. He began with a familiar illustration. "Which of you," he asked while staring into a fire, filled with the smoke of fish cooking… *"which of you, if his son asks for bread, will give him a stone? Or if he asks for a fish, will give him a snake?"* (Matt 7:9,10)

The example took on a more intimate feeling in this place, where the stars filled the heavens, clearly. Every other time Jeshua used it was with the people in the light of day, their eyes reflecting their hunger to soak up his words as comfort. Our need was different. I spoke up.

"Master," I interrupted. "Why then, do some receive while others, apparently no less righteous struggle on in their pain?" Jeshua looked up at me, his eyes tender, expressing approval at the question. He looked again into the fire and continued. "You will remember that I asked Malachi how long his son had been in his condition. Malachi had answered, 'from childhood'. Do you really think a demon had entered this innocent little boy?" I was more than a little shocked. I had heard what I thought were the demons speaking. No, I had seen it. The foaming at the mouth, the convulsions. Jesus continued. "This generation seeks signs and wonders. Tell me, what led the people into the desert to see the Baptist? His fine clothes?" Jeshua smiled at his joke.

"No, I tell you, it was for Elijah they searched. What do they seek from me? Healing? No, food for their stomachs, like Moses of old. They seek one who will deliver them from Rome, from their poverty."

At that moment, the Master stood and we with him. "I tell you the truth. They have seen Elijah and Moses!" I glanced around to Peter and James. Jeshua continued. "All things are possible for those who believe, who truly follow the way of Yahweh. My Father desires to give His life to all who will come. I am that life. I am that way. But we can come only to those who believe, those who see in both their good and bad the purposes of my Father, those who remain open to life, like a child."

Jesus turned to leave us, for prayer, we assumed. He had not walked twenty feet's distance when he turned back. "That is what I meant when I said, 'This kind can come only by prayer.' This disease did not come upon Jacob without purpose…" With that Jeshua turned once again. But my mind quickly filled in the rest. *'Ask and it will be given you; seek and you will find; knock and the door will be opened'* (Matthew 7:7,8).

Reflections on "Faith Unpacked"

"One of my favorite moments with Jeshua and the twelve is when we are alone and able to unpack the day's events, the questions, the failures..." John

Q: Do you have such a moment built into your life? ...A time to unpack the day's events, the questions, the failures; with Jesus or within yourself?

Q: Does your church have such moments? ...where?

Turn your thoughts to pen or prayer.

Week-2: SUNDAY—MATTHEW 5:3 & 6:25-27 & 8:14-17 & II CORINTHIANS 11:24-30 & 12:7-10

MY THOUGHTS 4—THE DANCE

> *"...We tend, however, to divide our past into good things to remember with gratitude and painful things to accept or forget. This way of thinking, which at first glance seems quite natural, prevents us from allowing our whole past to be the source from which we live our future. It locks us into a self-involved focus on our gain or comfort. It becomes a way to categorize, and in a way, control. Such an outlook becomes another attempt to avoid facing our suffering."*
> Henri Nouwen, in "Turn My Mourning Into Dancing", page #15-17

Nouwen calls it a dance; a perfect metaphor to describe the tension of joy and pain, depression and self-direction, wounds and healing, ignorance and wisdom…of that gnawing awareness of willful sin lurking just beneath our deep and loving commitment to Jesus, much like a manufacturing plant unloading it's drops of crude into a crystal clear lake.

Like the yin/yang of eastern thought Christian mystics have always honored this tension and urged Jesus followers to authentically lay it all out before Jesus and confessionally God's church and certainly ourselves in the interior life we live.

If we embrace with gratitude all of life, as Nouwen argues, then we are in the rhythms of an eternal and joy-pain filled dance.

"And true gratitude embraces all of life: the good and the bad, the joyful and the painful, the holy and the not-so-holy. We do this because we become aware of God's life, God's presence in the middle of all that happens."
Henri Nouwen, in "Turn My Mourning Into Dancing", page #15-17

Reflections on "The Dance"

In II CORINTHIANS 11:24-30 & 12:7-10 Paul integrates glory and suffering, mission and his own weakness.

Q: What is the greatest gift you bring to any table? ...What is the vulnerable or broken or wounded space which can bring you or others down?

Q: Where is the glory of God clearly seen in your life? ...in your gifting or your broken spaces now being healed?

Reflect and perhaps turn it to a prayer.

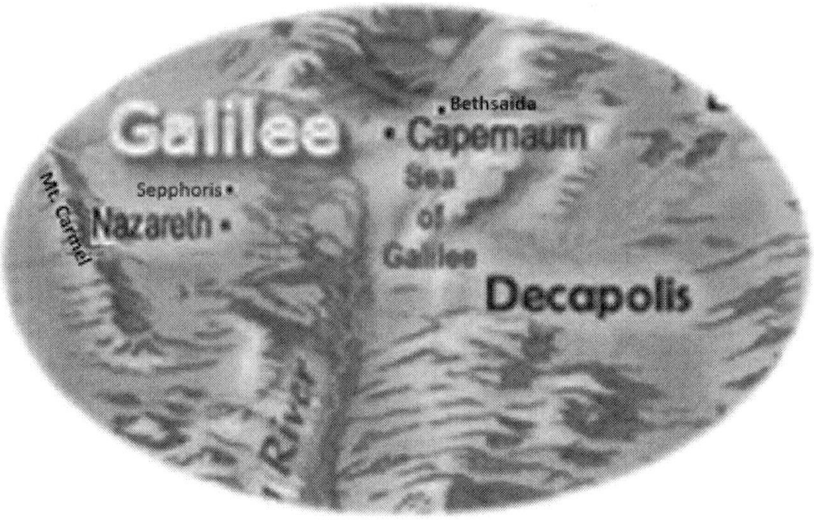
Bethsaida
Galilee
Capernaum
Sea
of
Galilee
Sepphoris
Nazareth
Mt. Carmel
Decapolis
River

3 Beyond Fear

...Recapturing Important Themes

Invocation:

Lord, make me an instrument of your peace. Where there is hatred, let me sow love; where there is injury, pardon; where there is doubt, faith; where there is despair, hope; where there is darkness, light; and where there is sadness, joy. O Divine Master, grant that I may not so much seek to be consoled as to console; to be understood as to understand; to be loved as to love.

For it is in giving that we receive; it is in pardoning that we are pardoned; and it is in dying that we are born to eternal life. Amen.

Prayer of St. Francis

Psalm of the Week: Psalm 15

Quote of the Week: It is our great illusion that life is a property to be owned or an object to be grasped, that people can be managed or manipulated.

From "Turn My Mourning into Dancing" by Henri Nouwen, pg #27

DAILY SCRIPTURES:

MONDAY—MATTHEW 6: 19-21 & 17: 24-27

TUESDAY—MATTHEW 6:28-34 & MARK 9: 38-41

WEDNESDAY—MATTHEW 7:1-6 & 9: 9-13
& MARK 9:33-37

THURSDAY—MATTHEW 5:3-10 & MARK 9: 42-50

FRIDAY—MATTHEW 6:14-15 & 18: 21-35 &
ISAIAH 50: 1-11

SATURDAY—MATTHEW 7: 13-14 & 18: 15-20

SUNDAY—MATTHEW 7:12 & 18:10-14 & EZEKIEL 34:11-16 & JOHN 10: 11-18

Rev. Terry Mattson

From
Turn My Mourning Into Dancing
by Henri Nouwen
Page #23

For years I have loved watching trapeze artists... At each performance they trust that their flight will end with their hands sliding into the secure grip of a partner. They also know that only the release of the secure bar allows them to move on with arcing grace to the next. Before they can be caught they must let go. They must brave the emptiness of space.

Living with this kind of willingness to let go is one of the greatest challenges we face. Whether it concerns a person, possession, or personal reputation, in so many areas we hold on at all costs. We become heroic defenders of our dearly gained happiness. We treat our sometimes inevitable losses as failures in the battle of survival.

The great paradox is that it is in letting go, we receive. We find safety in unexpected places of risk. And those who try to avoid all risk, those who would try to guarantee that their hearts will not be broken, end up in a self-created hell.

Week-3: MONDAY—MATTHEW 6: 19-21 & 17: 24-27
STORY 11—THE CATCH

The nets were exploding! Peter was barking orders. "John! Go to the stern and pull from there. James!" who was in our papa's other boat, not ten feet away, was working, together with my papa's hired hands, to keep the boats parallel. "James! Now!" Peter continued, his voice hoarse from the hours of yelling at us, the fish and the sea, sometimes cajoling, sometimes demanding, was still full of joy. At Peter's command, James maneuvered his boat so that a triangle was formed, allowing us to concentrate our energies on one end of the net and pull the fish into Peter's boat. "What a catch…" Peter laughed, as he had not since the day he left fishing to follow Jeshua.

For the next hour we worked to bring the catch to shore. Three hundred fifty-three in all. Enough to pay our father's debts and taxes. Peter was the first out of the boat. He grabbed for the first fish within reach and taking his knife, slit the fish open from head to tail. His eyes widened and then as suddenly filled with tears, from joy or sorrow I could not make out. All that he said, looking up into the heavens was, "Forgive me, papa, forgive me." All I could think of was Jeshua's own words, earlier that week. *"Which of you, if his son asks for bread, will give him a stone? Or if he asks for a fish, will give him a snake?"* (Matthew 7:9,10). I realized anew, that Jeshua knew our needs even before we asked.

The miracle of the catch and of the fishing began as we first came into the city, about the eighth hour of the day. Walking into Capernaum brought back a flood of memories for me and my cousins. Capernaum was the commercial center of my papa's fishing business.

Capernaum is nestled on the northwest shore of Galilee. She stands at the cross roads of the world, ancient and modern. Travelers from Persia or Greece, on their way to Egypt, would enter the Holy land here at Capernaum. Rome's rule over the territories recognized its importance by paving the Appian Way, the main highway from Damascus, through this city, around the sea and then east, up into the hill country near Sepphoris, toward the Great Sea. Matthew's tax business had been located on this highway, a perfect place to capture the taxes of both local businesses and travelers doing commerce.

Capernaum was also significant to the Jewish people. It boasted of the largest and visually the most inspiring of synagogues. Capernaum's rabbi and scribes were well connected with the elders in Jerusalem. Collections for the temple tax flowed from every son and daughter of Israel around Galilee into its sanctuary court yard.

Beyond that, the olive oil industry for all of Galilee, Samaria and Judea was centered here. Olive oil, pure and virgin, represented the anointing presence of Yahweh. Capernaum was filled with millstones to which were brought only the finest olives in Galilee, all grown in the orchards nestled around the sea. They were crushed in the Gethsemane's of Capernaum and stored for shipment, by way of the Sea of Galilee. It was no accident that Jeshua chose Capernaum as the center of his ministry, since the early days.

We had come into the city from the north, using the Appian Way. My own soul was ready for the respite of the city. While here, we would stay in Matthew's home, lavish by comparison, to any of the other disciples. Matthew had closed, not sold, his collection business and paid back fourfold those he had cheated in excessive and coercive tax collections over the years. The rest of his income was made available to the Master and that included his home.

As we passed by Matthew's old business, Peter walked up beside me. "Filthy wretches!" he whispered. "Peter!" I scolded. "Matthew was such a wretch at one time." Peter mumbled an apology, knowing his spirit was wrong. He then went on to confide in me. "John, you are right. Still, I speak with reason." I stopped, turned and looked at Peter intently. Peter drew close and spoke in a whisper as one speaks to a confident. The other ten went on their way, oblivious of our pause.

"Your papa, Zebedee," Peter began, hesitantly. My interest peaked. "When we came into Bethsaida last week, your papa took me aside and said that the business does not go well. With our absence, the hired replacements…" He paused, searching for words. "John," he continued, placing his hands on my shoulders. "Zebedee needs our help. He owes Rome and is unable to pay." My heart sank. Peter then turned me around so that I was again facing Capernaum and placing his arm around my shoulder, walked me toward the Synagogue for prayer. The ninth hour approached and with it, time for prayer.

As we entered into the court yard of the synagogue, with its high colonnades surrounding, we were approached by a scribe, apparently from Jerusalem. He had been sitting at the Temple tax booth just inside the courtyard and near the entrance of the synagogue. He evidently recognized Peter as being with Jesus. *"Doesn't your teacher pay the temple tax?"* he asked, pointing toward the Master who was just entering the sanctuary (Matthew 17: 22b). Peter's eyes glared into the scribe. Afraid a curse or worse was coming, I broke in. *"Of course he does!"* Peter relaxed a little and mumbled an affirmation and then moved past the scribe toward the others. My own heart was still heavy from Peter's news of papa's business. I knew that I had abandoned my papa to follow the Baptist and then Jeshua. I desperately needed to pray.

At about the twelfth hour we were all settled into Matthew's home. I was in despair. Peter was a little angry still at the seeming injustice of both Roman and Jewish taxes. Both of us kept our distance. The other ten were unaware of our feelings or our conversation about taxes and tax collectors.

Jeshua, pulling us out of ourselves, spoke up, addressing Peter. Knowing him well, he asked, "What do you think, Simon?" Jeshua's use of Peter's Jewish name was his way of reminding Peter of his human weakness. *"From whom do the kings of the earth collect duty and taxes—from their own sons or from others?" "From others,"* Peter answered. *"Then,"* Jeshua continued, *"the sons are exempt"* (Matthew 17: 25b-26).

Peter got the message and smiled. Jeshua continued. *"But so that we may not offend them, go to the lake and throw out your line. Take the first fish you catch; open its mouth and you will find a four-drachma coin. Take it and give it to them for my tax and yours"* (Matthew 17: 27).

Peter need not be told a second time. Fishing was never far from his heart. Signaling me, James and Andrew, he stood to leave. We followed and made our way down to the sea, to the commercial docks where our boats were stored. It would be a night of fishing.

Reflections on "The Catch"

Reflecting on Matthew 6: 19-21, consider:

Q: How much do you worry about money? ...Why?

Q: Does your worry represent a 'lack of trust' or some

thing else? ...What else?

Describe a time when God saved you financially and turn it all to thanksgiving in prayer:

Week-3: TUESDAY—MATTHEW 6:28-34 & MARK 9: 38-41
MY THOUGHTS 5—DRIVEN OR CREATIVE

my thoughts

"It is our great illusion that life is a property to be owned or an object to be grasped, that people can be managed or manipulated."
From "Turn My Mourning into Dancing" by Henri Nouwen, "Life's Great Illusion," Page #27-29

I love all things Star Trek. One of my all-time favorite episodes of the original Trek was when the Enterprise picked up a 21st century (old earth dating) pre-warp space ship loaded with persons who were dying and chose cryogenics in the hope of being re-awakened in the distant future when their disease could be healed.

One of the men who had been frozen and now brought back to life was driven and used to giving orders, a Donald Trump kinda guy on steroids. He was generally making himself a nuisance to Captain Kirk and the mission to which the Enterprise was committed, requiring Kirk to put him in his place. Which he did. This once rich business man explained that his demanding behavior was the result of, for the first time in his life, not being in control now that he lived in a world where his money no longer mattered. After explaining that this bright new world allowed every person, rich and poor, the freedom to explore and learn and become, he asked Kirk, "What's the point of living if I can't fight and scratch and make my way by power and money, to control my own destiny?" to which Kirk responded, "That kind of control is an illusion."

And it is! Always has been. Life is not created for those who knowing the art of the deal demand, shove and push but for those who remain open to all the nuances of life, its joys and suffering to the end that we discover God and God's love in all.

This closing Jesus narrative presents to the twelve and now to us a choice; Is life all about control or a freely given responsiveness to life as God gives it. Peter was rebuked by Jesus precisely because he told Jesus he must now allow his capture and suffering. Nouwen notes that in these last weeks "the phrase 'handed over'" was used time and again by the gospel writers "to refer to Jesus and his followers." In this phrase, the gospels remind these first century persons, many who were slaves or poor or persecuted (and us) that we are not made to control but to creatively respond to life, seeking only love.

Reflections on "Driven or Creative"

"God handed his son over for our sins. Jesus no longer was the One who preached, spoke, healed, took the initiative. What was done, was done to him. He was spit upon, led to the cross, flagellated, crucified. The Word, the One through whom all is created now becomes a victim of his creation. That is what his death meant—being out of control, for our sakes, from great love."

From "Turn My Mourning into Dancing" Henri Nouwen, "Life's Great Illusion," Page #27-29

Q: Do you tend to be 'driven' or 'responsive'? ...What makes the difference in you?

Q: What is the primary motivation in your life—Love, power, money, pleasure, prestige? ...How so?

Reflect and perhaps turn it to a prayer.

Week-3: WEDNESDAY—Matthew 7:1-6 & 9: 9-13
& Mark 9:33-37

Story 12—Unfinished Business

We were all pretty relaxed, sitting around the open fire pit in the center of Matthew's incredible home. This was the very home that most of us had once refused to enter, scandalized at the very thought of Jesus under Matthew's roof, by invitation. So deeply had Matthew, the tax collector, been moved by Jesus' teaching that he invited him to his home for a celebration. Mary Magdalene was often an invited guest, her amorous sensibilities prized by Matthew and his friends. We had tried to dissuade Jesus. "Master," I had said., "Matthew is worse than a pagan. What goes on under his roof, I dare not say. You cannot go in there. All of Capernaum will abandon you!" All Jesus could say was, *"I have not come to call the righteous, but sinners."* Then he added. "Why don't you come? It should be fun" (Matthew 9: 13b).

That was three years ago. Now Matthew was one of us and also Mary, who often stayed with us. And so, here we were, former enemies, reconciled by love, enjoying an evening respite from the gathering storm that had surrounded us since Peter's confession and our master's revelation of approaching sorrow. Laughter filled our celebration as Peter recounted, for all, the story of yesterday's catch and the fish with four coins in his stomach. He mimed the fishes mouth while demonstrating how it wiggled to hide the treasure it had caught. Two children, huddled near Jeshua, one on his lap, began clapping at the play. I recognized them as the children of one of Matthew's friends, still a paid Roman tax collector. 'My,' I thought, 'how we have changed in three years.' Jeshua joined in the clapping, as did we all.

Jeshua spoke up as the laughter subsided. "Peter," he said, somewhat playfully. "Tell me, a few days ago, as we made our way up into the hills above Capernaum. You seemed rather angry about some teasing, telling everyone to shut up, as I recall. Of what were you arguing?"

Suddenly, our laughter stopped. We looked at each other and then Jeshua..., in disbelief. Peter, rather awkwardly, glancing around for an escape, moved from the center by the fire, to take his seat and buy some time before answering. Andrew saved him. "Brother, you look as white as a fish, caught with coins in his mouth!" The tension broke as we all laughed. Peter looked relieved and Jeshua, smiling, lifted the child from his lap up into his arms and took the other with his hand and came into the center of the circle. "These children," he began, "Rebecca and Joshua, have enjoyed the evening, as have we all. They do not care what your trade is; whether you are a fisherman or mason, a rabbi or tax collector." Quickly, I glanced over at their papa, who was a tax collector, as did Matthew. "Nor are they concerned with who among us is powerful and who serves." Taking Rebecca and tossing her around him, holding her by the arms and letting her feet fly, he placed her near her brother, Joshua and continued. "Nor do they care who is first to eat or last. They only want to love and be loved. To laugh and play and learn." Then, placing himself between the children, with his hands on their heads, he added. "And that is what it means to live in my papa's house, where everyone is welcome. Everyone is invited to play and laugh and weep." Looking at Andrew. "Andrew, why do you care if Peter and James and John sit on my right or my left, or on my lap?"

Jeshua smiled and looked straight at Rebecca, who was giggling at the thought of Peter on Jeshua's lap. "Andrew, if you wish to be great, welcome a child into your heart and love as she does. Then you will be truly great, for *whoever welcomes one of these children in my name, welcomes me"* (Mark 9: 37).

Then Jeshua took the children to their father and greeted him warmly, and left into the darkness, we assumed to pray. We returned to our conversations and eating. I looked up at Jeshua, as he was walking out into the night and wondered, 'perhaps we have not changed so much, as yet.'

Note: This story is based, in part, upon scene in "Jesus of Nazareth"

Reflections on "Unfinished Business"

Review again, Matthew 7: 1-6 and consider the freedom Jesus is inviting you to know:

Q: Do you worry about others in relation to you? ...Why? ...Why not?

Q: Does judgment come easily to your mind or your lips?

Allow Jesus to approach you about the unfinished business in your life.

Q: What would he say or do?

Write it out or pray it out.

Week-3: THURSDAY—Matthew 6:9-13 & Mark 9: 42-50

My Thoughts 6—Leaving our Compulsions Behind

"To be converted fully is to let God lead us out of our compulsions. It means that we admit how we give up ceaselessly trying to 'fix' things. Freedom is the opposite of compulsive obsessions.

From "Turn My Mourning into Dancing" by Henri Nouwen, "Leaving our Compulsions Behind," Page #30-31

The gift of childhood is great desire mingled with light attachments and little worry.

I remember my first trip to Disney Land. I was standing just inside the main gate, past the little round park to the entrance of Main street just beyond the train which had taken us all around the park with my eyes ever widening as I saw the little cars, the submarine and the Matterhorn. I could not wait to get in and explore.

And now, as I looked down and into what to a child was the longest street ever and filled with candy canes, cotton candy, chocolate, shakes, burgers and toys my eyes widened further. It was going to be a magical day in The Magical Kingdom.

The responsive joy of that little boy has faded with the arrival of obsessive attachment; addictive longings for all the exciting and legitimate wonders that fill the magical kingdom of the earth. Now it is the longing, the hit, the rush of adrenaline that replaces what once was simple experience;

as relationships become possessive and what was once simply touch, taste, smell are diminished by hunger for ever more sensations unrelated to what makes them magical. What is worse is that each experience, when driven by ever deepening longing pressed by fantasy, is actually less exciting, less of a rush. And so the stakes are raised.

In Capernaum, standing next to a Gethsemane, that crushing and rounded stone that produced the best olive oil and wine in Galilee, Jesus spoke movingly of addiction as a heavy stone around the neck, especially of anyone who robbed a child not yet addicted to the innocent magic to be found on Main street.

Reflections on "Leaving our Compulsions Behind"

"To be converted fully is to let God lead us out of our compulsions…This is not easy, of course, mostly because intense needs motivate us. We feel lonely, for example, and thereby look—sometimes desperately— for someone who can take away the pain: a husband, wife, friend. We are all too ready to conclude that someone or something can finally take away our neediness".

From "Turn My Mourning into Dancing" by Henri Nouwen, "Leaving our Compulsions Behind," Page #30-31

Q: What is your greatest need? …Forgiveness or conversion?

Q: To be free, to become a child again would look like what?

Turn your thoughts and heart to God, in hope.

Week-3: FRIDAY—MATTHEW 6:14-15 & 18: 21-35 & ISAIAH 50: 1-11

STORY 11—LOVING BEYOND FEAR

It was the Sabbath. The synagogue was filled. Word of Jesus presence had brought out everyone. Each had their own reasons. Some were curious, some came out of love or devotion and still others to find a way to trap him. Many were simply present in promise of a show. The synagogue was deeply divided over Jesus, as was the nation.

The rabbi, respected by all the people and by Jeshua, invited Jesus to comment of the readings of the prophet Isaiah. Jeshua turned the scroll carefully to the prepared text and began to read.

> *"Where is your mother's certificate of divorce*
> *with which I sent her away?*
> *Or to which of my creditors did I sell you?"*
> Isaiah 50: 1a

My mind began to drift as I looked about me, watching with interest the response on each face. *'And you, Capernaum, will you be lifted up to the skies? No, you will go down to the depths.'* My mind suddenly saw this moment in Yahweh's synagogue from heaven's perspective. 'They don't get it!' Jeshua's words continued in my heart. *'If the miracles that were performed in you had been performed in Sodom, it would have remained to this day'* (Matthew 11:23). My heart felt as though it were breaking. 'These were the ones Jeshua was referring to. Their outcome may be worse than the judgment of Yahweh upon Sodom and Gomorrah… 'How can that be?' I fretted, 'We are the children of covenant!'

Suddenly my mind was brought back by the words of the prophet. Jeshua's voice hesitated. He looked into the crowd, at the elders who had traveled from Jerusalem. They often seemed to appear out of nowhere, as though following. His voice grew intense, quiet, yet with determination he continued, from memory.

> *"I offered my back to those who beat me,*
> *my cheeks to those who pulled out my beard:*
> *I did not hide my face from mocking and spitting.*
> *Because the Sovereign LORD helps me;*
> *I will not be disgraced."*
> Isaiah 50: 6-7a

I stared into Jeshua's eyes. The Words of Isaiah drove deeply into my heart, like a nail pounded into the flesh of the wicked upon a Roman cross. 'Was this a prophecy of my Lord, of Jeshua? Is this the end of our mission to which Jeshua referred at Mt. Herman?' I buried my head in my hands as I listened, intently.

> *"Let us face each other!*
> *Who is my accuser? Let him confront me!*
> *It is the sovereign LORD who helps me.*
> *Who is he that condemn me?"*
> Isaiah 50: 8b-9a

I looked up and into Jeshua's face. He had not turned away from staring at the elders as he recited that passage. Until now. Jeshua, again looked at the text and continued the reading. I turned my head toward the elders. They sat in stone silence, revealing nothing. How my heart yearned within me, as I came face to face with the fear and hatred of these elders of Israel. I heard nothing else, till Jeshua began his comments.

Slowly Jeshua rolled up the scroll, lifted it to his lips and kissed the sacred text. He then placed the scroll on the podium before him. "Today, he began slowly. "This day my Papa and yours has shed his garments."

Jeshua was painting the picture of God's final rejection of Israel's sin, I feared. By the rendering of a garment a priest or elder dramatizes their agony over some great wound or sin. "In earnest.," Jeshua continued, "not in anger, but in sadness." I lifted my head waiting for the words to come. Words, which I knew could well be his last, if he offended too deeply. "In the wilderness as Moses led our people from bondage in Egypt, did Yahweh ever abandon us? Or in the time of Solomon's many sins, though grieved, did not my Papa keep faith with Israel? Was it not Yahweh who instructed the prophet Hosea to remain faithful to a harlot, in demonstration of his great love?"

Jeshua moved to the side of the lectern, every eye fixed upon him. "Where is the certificate of divorce? When have I sent you away from me?" Jeshua, placed his hand upon a child nearby. "I tell you, it is not my Father's love which wavers. It is not His passion which fails. It is ours sins which separates us from His presence, just as a child's chord is cut at birth. Such is the cost of our sin!"

"Do not fear God's wrath. Rather fear your own self, caught in the snare of Lucifer's net and thrown into the sea, left to drown. I say, fear Yahweh's mercy, which allows such as these..." Jeshua stopped and picked up the child in his arms before continuing. *"And if anyone causes one of these little ones who believe in me to sin, it would be better for him to be thrown into the sea..."* Jeshua walked over to the archway opening out to the courtyard, and continued more softly. *"It would be better for him to be thrown into the sea with a large millstone around his neck."* Turning back, he continued. "Do not fear God's wrath. Rather fear your own self. *If your hand causes you to sin, cut it off. It is better for you to enter life maimed than with two hands to go to hell. And if your eye causes you to stumble, pluck it out. It is better to enter the kingdom of God with one eye than to have two eyes and be thrown into hell"* (selections in italic are Mark 9: 42-50).

Jeshua placed the child again on the ground near his own papa and continued: "My Papa's kingdom is a place of forgiveness, deep and wide, like the sea. But woe to the one who misuses this gift." Jeshua moved toward the front of the podium. "The love of my Papa is like a great Lord who demanded payment in full from all his creditors. And so…" Jeshua took a seat just below the podium and spoke as if to each person. "And so a very poor man was brought before him, from debtor's prison. Now this poor man owed the Lord one million dollars. Never could he pay it back. "Take pity on me, the poor man cried." And the Lord of that country, in great love, took pity and forgave the man all that he owed and restored him to his home, his family. Now, sometime later, the poor man came into need of some money to buy a gift for his wife. He called in every man who owed him anything. Some, who owed him pennies and others who owed a few dollars. "Pay me what you owe, now, or I shall throw you into debtor's prison." The man who owed him just a few pennies cried out. "My Lord, take pit on me." But the poor man had no pity and ordered him thrown into prison to rot, until someone would come to pay his debt." Jeshua stood and moved toward one of the elders from Jerusalem. "Now some time passed. Word of the plight of this very poor man living in debtor's prison came to the attention of the Lord of the land. When the Lord heard his plight and who it was that left him to rot in prison, he called the poor back before him. "So you thought my mercy was a gift for you alone, did you? Take him from me. Sell all he has and give it to the very poor man who owed him pennies and throw this worthless servant into a debtor's prison, from which there is no escape!" Looking straight into the face of one of the elders, Jeshua continued, softly. "So I tell you plainly. It is not my Papa's wrath you need to fear. But His mercy! If you love, you will be given love. If you hate, you will be given more hate than you know what to do with."

Reflections on "Loving Beyond Fear"

Terry suggests in this story that it is not fear of God's wrath, but fear of the Father's love that should concern us.

Q: How does this thought strike you?

Q: What does he mean? ...Does it ring true?

Q: Based on this narrative, what is hell?

Turn your thoughts into prayer for yourself or others...to avoid the clutches of a self-created hell.

Week-3: SATURDAY—MATTHEW 7: 13-14 & 18: 15-20

MY THOUGHTS 7—MOVING BEYOND FEAR

my thoughts

"Those who can make us afraid have power over us. Those who make us live in a house of fear ultimately take our freedom away".
From "Turn My Mourning into Dancing" by Henri Nouwen, "Moving out of the House of Fear," Page #32-34

We are a people afraid. Fear driven anger enshrines our 2015-2016 political debates. We are apparently prepared to nominate to national office a political novice whose identity is all about power in order to feel safe; to erect a wall to keep them out and send them packing, take their oil and shoot them dead. Will we be safer? Perhaps. But we will also be less free, a people filled with anxious loneliness as we withdraw from the world, build up fortress America only to come out when threatened and take em down.

It is the very 'them' or 'em' whom we fear that changes us into an image of the ones we feel victimized by. That is the nature of fear. It walls you in, behind closed doors and hearts, cut off, alone.

The twelve disciples would soon enough be frozen by fear. It already begins to echo in their thoughts and feelings as they sense the us verses them rising as they slowly make their way to Jerusalem. Thomas expresses it as they gather their belongings to go to within miles of Jerusalem to comfort Martha and Mary in their loss of Lazarus, *"Let us also go, that we may die with him"* (John 11: 16b). This same fear would send them running from a garden called Gethsemane as they felt the crushing weight of Caiaphas's troops descend upon them.

And what is the antidote? It is love. Only one problem. They would have to be willing to die for love's sake. Peter declared he was willing to fight. I think he was. And he proved it as he went into the enemy's camp following Jesus arrest. But he could not muster up the courage to lay down his life in love as his master was doing and so he curses in anger at a servant girl, lost in a small crowd gathered near a crackling fire.

And us? We have not changed so much. Today we fight our evangelical battles over 'our place' within the political-social-cultural America, keenly aware that we are losing that battle. We are afraid and angry. Like Peter, we are fighting the wrong battle and our fear driven sense of isolation from our culture proves it.

Reflections on "Moving Beyond Fear"

> *"Wherever we live, the invitation of Christ beckons us to move out of the house of fear into the house of love: to leave our possessiveness for a place of freedom The Word became flesh and pitched its tent among us so that God could dwell in the house of love among us..."*
> From "Turn My Mourning into Dancing" by Henri Nouwen, "Moving out of the House of Fear," Page #32-34

Terry suggests the evangelical church has not come so very far. That we are perhaps closer to the twelve disciples in their Jerusalem journey than we are to Christ.

Q: What do you think? ...Is he right?

Q: What would love (as opposed to fear) look like in your church in your community?

The say actions speak louder than words:

Q: Do you generally live closer to fear or love? ...How So? ...Why?

Speak to God of your fears. Listen for God's love in response.

Week-3: SUNDAY—MATTHEW 7:12 & 18:10-14 & EZEKIEL 34:11-16 & JOHN 10: 11-18

MY THOUGHTS 8—BORN OF FEAR; BOURN BY LOVE

This poem was written to my son on the eve of his graduation from college: It is intended as a biographical sketch of his journey inside ours as;

- A memory from his birth
- A baby when I was a youth minister
- A young child when I struggled with sin
- A preacher's kid in the season of restoration in ministry
- A high school student in a private school
- A young adult in his first love
- A college student at NNU
- A graduate
- A reflection from his birth

Who Am I?

Born of fear; Bourn by Love
Re-born in Love

The ugliest baby I had ever seen,
  I remember well my first impressions.

A dark wrinkled gray little baby,
    silent to the world,
        was placed on her stomach,
      for seconds only,
   till the chord to her womb was broken,
    never to be restored.

In silence they worked,
    doctor and nurse,
        urgent and quick,
        no celebration or panic,
   the feel of a birth at risk,

It all seemed,
        surreal.
  Why did I not feel pride of birth?
    Or;
    hear the slap of bottom
    and lungs filling with the sounds of primordial
    scream?
  Only a limp,
    grayish and lifeless form.
  I remember the guilt as I wondered,
    at the picture before me,
      unaware of just how
      near death's door you brushed.

Within seconds, they pulled you from us;
    Turning their backs,
        poking and probing for signs of life.
    The nurse, our friend,
            rushed you out of the room.
            Suddenly aware I was,
                something was wrong,
            from the start.

Fear followed this child, of our dreams…
Loved at first by mother and father;
    Soon to be the child of our teens,
    tossed to one and then another,
        passed around,
        cuddled and held,
        fawned over like those,
        who are special,
    the center of our little world.

Then came my wandering years,
    another child,
        and my focus forever changed,
    from Shaun
    to the wounded spaces in others,
      My own and ours.

God gave a teacher,
  wise as she was old,
    Ms. Plaisted her name,
    she felt your fear and gave you place.

Your mother held you
    and watched you grow.

Your anger came and I feared the worst,
>   but my own sins loomed large,
>   and so I watched from just outside,
>   the life of a tender little boy,
>   whose dreams were large,
>   explore in a world of basketball,
>   your talent unequal to the task.

I feared, for you,
>   but still held you at bay,
>   even as the renewal of my mission,
>   promised hope of a new day.

God gave two grandmothers,
>   whose hearts knew only love.
>   They gave you a safe place
>   for adventures of the mind,
>   with cousins and ice cream,
>   with hamburgers and fries, they kept you apart.

Then came Seattle,
>   a city diverse,
A world without the safety of God, being first.
You reeled as the fears took hold,
>   Your anger increased.
>   I was fully present,
>   but too driven to see,
>   my absence,
>   first in sin and now in mission,
>   left you alone on the street.

God gave you men,
>   who shared your love of sport,
>   who saw raw talent

and could awaken it on court.
These men shared my vision,
of a world without fear and loved you...
as my prayers made me keenly aware,
    just how absent I had been.

A promise God made,
in this season of silence.
    You he would save,
        and your children after,
        for at least three generations,
    if only I would follow.

In fear you were born and in fear re-born;
    Your God was angry with sin,
    But for you he came to win.
        He looked good in the skin,
        of young women from afar,
    Here was a world you knew.
It was safe and the rules seemed secure.
God gave you a school,
    A place where Christ was still a star.
    Your desire to excel
    found expression in your heart.
In worship and in Church,
among teens your own age you found,
    Another calling and the grace to abound.
    You dreamed,
     mostly inside your skills and found the power of
    preaching,
        the promises of God.
    You searched for other places
      where God's Spirit seemed real,
The hole inside you grew,

Who Am I?

    Even as I challenged your
    theological positions.

God gave you a world;
A church in which He lived,
    inside the conflicts and broken
    spaces of people
      who at first, you did not see,
          were a whole lot like you.

You loved and risked,
An adventure begun turned into a nightmare,
From which one love died,
    another begun.
    Inside this empty longing,
    you found assurance first;
        The courage to face clearly,
          The you inside brokenness.
        You looked anew at life,
        her joys and sorrows bourn.
   Two kingdoms vied for power,
    One love,
        one certainty.

God brought you into college,
To a place where studies were real,
    He gave a place of service,
     Your heart felt more than a little.
      You tasted the beginnings of love,
        still unknown.

You stumbled as do all men,
    But were not afraid to face
    the demons scorn.

God gave You Love,
                His, no more.
He graced you with friends, plenty.
    Different places each,
    you learned.

He gave you a woman fine,
      whose heart is sweet like wine,
      The question slowly formed.
          Is God love,
              really love?
              Is the holy always love?

God gave you a community
      in which to learn
      Of a vision, called hope.
      Of a world He is making,
      An invitation always open.

You have allowed this love to hold you,
      And felt your sorrow grow,
      As salvation became sanctification,
      And prayers were slowly filled.

You are moving beyond the fear
    into which you were born,
Yours and mine and your Church's,
    All human, never alone.

God gave you talent, plenty,
      For the task to which He calls.
      He invites you into eternity,
      His, where love transforms.

Who Am I?

I remember that very first night,
    Not twenty minutes had passed.
    They had poked and prodded,
    Using pain to awaken you,
        by fear.
        I stood by,
            alone,
                mom in another place.
I wept inside, God why?
        Why is this necessary?
        ...on his very first day?
    Finally, the doctors stopped,
    The nurses too and walked away,
    Content they were,
        that you would live to at least,
        day two.
    I stepped up to your side,
    Screaming you were,
                all alone.
Shaun, I spoke your name.
    I took your hand,
    your little hand clasped my finger.
    I began my first sermon,
    To this little boy of my heart.
        I sang a song that I had,
While you lay near your mother's heart.
    Jesus loves you, this I know,
  For the Bible tells me so.
    Little ones to him belong,
    they are weak, but He is strong.
        Yes, Jesus loves you.
        Yes, Jesus loves you.
    Yes, Jesus loves you.
        The Bible tells me so.

As the sound of my voice filled the air,
> My little boy, silent became,
> There were no more tears.

Born into a world of pain,
> yes, you are.
But there is only one power known
> That calms this fear.
> > It is the love of Jesus who moves us,
> > > Beyond fear.

Love, dad,
May 8, 2010
...on the night before your graduation.

Reflections on "Born of fear; Bourn by Love"

Since this writing, nearly six years have passed. My son is now my pastor and in the church in which he was raised.

His message is one of love, powerfully delivered in sermon and by pastoral leadership. Still, it is a message he is learning to live… for fear, in him as in all, remains.

Q: Can you identify with Shaun's story in poem? …that life is a passage from fear to love?

Reflect on your own journey in and to love. Write your story and then pray and give thanks.

Map of Galilee region showing Capernaum, Sea of Galilee, Sepphoris, Nazareth, Mt. Carmel, Beth Shean, Decapolis, Caesarea, Samaria, Peraea, and the Jordan River.

4 Facing South

...on the Journey to Jerusalem

Invocation:

Lord, we have labored all day, but we fear all is lost. And it is, unless, You join our labor with Your love. We rise early. Rise with us. We retire late. Help us to unwind from the day. Speak, Lord. Help us to listen. Our work, Lord, is hard. Give us Your broken body and renew us. We sleep... Let us rest in peace. Let even our dreams be a reflection of Your care. Amen.

Adapted from Psalm 127: 1-2

Psalm of the Week: Psalm 128

Quote of the Week: "As we make God the center of our lives, our sense of who we are will depend less on what others think of or say about us. We will cease being prisoners of the interpersonal."

From "Turn My Mourning into Dancing" by Henri Nouwen, pg #34

DAILY SCRIPTURES:

MONDAY—MATTHEW 5: 31-32 & 19: 1-12 & LUKE 15: 1-7

TUESDAY—MATTHEW 7: 24-27 & 19: 13-15

WEDNESDAY—MATTHEW 5: 43-45 & 19: 16-22 & JOHN 9:1-5

THURSDAY—MATTHEW 5: 48 & 6: 19-21 & MARK 10: 23-31

FRIDAY—MATTHEW 5: 33-37 & 20: 1-16

SATURDAY—MATTHEW 5: 11-12 & MARK 10: 32-34

SUNDAY—MATTHEW 5: 13 & LUKE 9: 51-55 & LUKE 12: 49-56 & JOHN 14: 25-27 & GALATIANS 2: 1-16 & 3: 26-28

Rev. Terry Mattson

Converting Illusions Through Prayer

From
Turn My Mourning Into Dancing
by Henri Nouwen
Page #34-35

Only prayer allows us to hear another voice, to respond to the larger possibilities, to find a way out of our need to order and control. Then the questions that seem to shape our identity will not matter so much. Who says good things about me? Who doesn't? Who is my friend? My enemy? How many like me? As we make God the center of our lives, our sense of who we are will depend less on what others think of or say about us. We will cease being prisoners of the interpersonal.

Indeed, prayer shows us how to keep the interpersonal from becoming an idol. It reminds us that we learn to love only because we have glimpsed or sensed a first love, a supreme love. Here is the way to a love that transcends the interpersonal: 'We love because he first loved us' (I John 4:19). We find freedom as we are touched by that first love. For it is that love that will break us away from our alienation and separation. It is a love that can soothe our compulsions to hoard and pretend we can organize the future. It is a love that allows us to love others.

Week-4: MONDAY—MATTHEW 5: 31-32 & 19: 1-12 & LUKE 15: 1-7

STORY 12—GATHERING STORM

I hugged my mama, Salome. She had come to Capernaum to see her boys, James and I, one more time before we left the area. She had also come to the Synagogue to surround us with prayer. Jeshua had left the courtyard of the Synagogue about an hour before, heading southeast. along the northern coast of the sea. A large crowd followed, women and children and men, young and old.

"I will be fine, mama. Don't worry yourself," I said as I released her embrace. "My son." She spoke in earnest, her hands cupping my face. "You are close to the Master. See that your brother is taken care of when Jesus comes into his kingdom." "Of course, mama, always." "And your papa and I shall see you at the festival in Jerusalem in a few Sabbaths," she continued, running past my assurance. With that, I turned from Mama to catch up with my Master. It would not be difficult. I was familiar with the areas surrounding Capernaum that Jeshua chose for mission. Besides, the crowd of followers numbered in the thousands. It would not be hard to find him. 'How,' I wondered, 'can anything happen to Jeshua? He is just too popular.' Then I remembered the looks of the Pharisees just moments earlier, as Jeshua spoke in the synagogue. Their countenance was different, somehow darker.

Just outside of Capernaum, not a mile in distance was a perfect place for teaching. Two hills, with a creek flowing between and into Galilee, formed a natural amphitheater. It was Jeshua's favorite place to teach when in Capernaum. As I crested the hill, before me was a crowd of a thousand or more. Jeshua sat, near the lake. To his left were a number of

Pharisees and Sadducees or scribes questioning him. But unlike earlier encounters, their questions, voices and postures seemed to express challenge, not inquiry. I had seen it before, in the later part of the Baptist's ministry. Fear seized me. My mama's hug suddenly seemed far away. Jeshua's words echoed in my ear. *'We are going up to Jerusalem and the Son of Man will be betrayed to the chief priests and the teachers of the law. They will condemn him to death and will turn him over to the Gentiles to be mocked and flogged and crucified'* (Matthew 20: 18,19b).

My troubled thoughts were interrupted by a Pharisee's voice, rising in intensity, something near anger. He was pointing toward Matthew's friend, Malchius, a tax collector, who continued to show great interest in Matthew's change of heart and the way of Jesus. "This man!" the Pharisee stood, his robes fluttering in the gentle breeze and his finger extended towards Malchius. "This man is worse than a pagan. You know him, for he is a good friend of your disciple Matthew, also a tax collector!" The Pharisee did not seem overly concerned with his facts. He paused, stroking his beard, allowing his words to hit their mark with the audience. "Tell me," Rabbi, his voice softened in feeling, though not volume. "Why do you welcome him? How many in this great crowd of your followers has he robbed?"

Malchius stood, his head bowed and reaching for his children, he prepared to leave. Jeshua reached out to caution Malchius. "Please stay. You are welcome!" Malchius took his seat out of respect, his face betraying the pain of staying. Jeshua stood and walked through and past the Pharisees and scribes gathered, almost brushing up against the one making the accusations. He positioned himself between them and the crowd, away from Malchius. I knew Jeshua well enough to know that he was simply refocusing the conversation away from Matthew's friend. He began to tell a story.

"Suppose one of you has a hundred sheep and loses one of them." Many of those listening had sheep or knew those who

did. *"Does he not leave the ninety-nine in the open country and go after the lost sheep until he finds it? And when he finds it, he joyfully puts it on his shoulders and goes home. Then he calls his friends and neighbors together and says, 'Rejoice with me; I have found my lost sheep.' I tell you.'* Jeshua turned back toward the accusing Pharisee. *'I tell you that in the same way there will be rejoicing in heaven over one sinner who repents than over the ninety-nine righteous persons who do not need to repent"* (Luke 15: 4-7). Looking straight at his accuser, he continued, his own voice softening. "Benjamin. You are a Pharisee, an elder among the people. Is it lawful for a man to divorce his wife for any and every reason?" (Matthew 19:3b).

I was now standing about half way down the hill. I sat down smiling. I did not want to distract, Jeshua had just turned the tables on the Pharisee. You see, the scribes who are Sadducees and the Pharisees were deeply divided over the appropriate place of divorce. The scribes, who function as priests and legal interpreters of the law had, over time, taken the position that any son of Abraham could divorce any daughter of Sarah for pretty much any reason. If a wife was lazy or seemed distant, it was reason enough. The Pharisees, on this issue, wanted to reserve divorce for especially severe marital issues. In one question Jesus had divided his accusers. Benjamin, recognizing the strategy simply turned the question back to Jeshua. "Please rabbi, tell us what you think?"

Smiling, Jeshua allowed his head to sway back, seeming to enjoy the debate. Looking around, I noticed the crowd was intent. A few were also smiling, watching the show. "Well then, since you ask," Jeshua began. *"Haven't you read,"* he replied, *"that at the beginning the Creator made them male and female,' and said, 'For this reason a man will leave his father and mother and be united to his wife, and the two will become one flesh'? So they are no longer two, but one. Therefore, what God has joined together, let man not separate"* (Matthew 19: 4-6).

A Sadducee in their troupe stood, taking the bait. *"Why then,* he asked, *"did Moses command that a man give his wife a certificate of divorce and send her away?"* Now Jesus turned directly to the scribe and responded. *"Moses permitted you to divorce your wives because your hearts were hard. But it was not this way from the beginning. I tell you that anyone who divorces his wife, except for marital unfaithfulness, and marries another woman commits adultery"* (Matthew 19: 7-9).

Then, turning back toward the crowd and moving up the creek and away from the scribes and Pharisees he continued. "All of my Papa's children, sons of Israel and sons of the pagans, farmers and soldiers, fisherman and tax collectors; All are welcome at his table, in his house." Jeshua came to a rock near the stream, sat down as if to emphasize his next point. "All of Papa's children have sinned and greatly. No one has fulfilled, in their heart, the commands of Moses. As the prophet says, we are like sheep, who have wandered." He looked down in a pause before continuing. "Listen to me. Truly listen. The only sin that will not be forgiven at the last day is the sin of a hard heart."

Rising and turning back toward the elders, Jeshua finished. "Yes, Moses allows for a separation from pain those whose hearts will not soften. But that is not what Yahweh intended." Moving to within a few feet of the scribe. "Keep faith with Yahweh's law. Keep faith with the wife of your youth. But do so in your heart and not just in words. Then divorce, will not be necessary."

Again, Jeshua turned once more and walking past the elders and over to Malchius, Matthew's friend, he took a seat and began to talk, as one does with a friend. Malchius smiled and offered him wine, which Jeshua freely took. Jeshua's message was done for the day. At least his words were done.

Reflections on "Gathering Storm"

Q: How does this story strike you? ...Can you imagine Jesus being both powerfully loving and combative?

> *"All of Papa's children have sinned and greatly. No one has fulfilled, in their heart, the commands of Moses. As the prophet says, we are like sheep, who have wandered...Listen to me. Truly listen. The only sin that will not be forgiven at the last day is the sin of a hard heart."*
>
> Jesus, as told from Johns memory & imagined by Terry

Terry picture's Jesus as getting to the heart of the matter in these words.

Consider this understanding of sin and grace and then ask:

Q: So, how hard or open is your heart to the will and movement of God?

Reflect and pray:

Week-4: TUESDAY—MATTHEW 7: 24-27 & 19: 13-15

MY THOUGHTS 9—GOD SURPRISES!

"Even in our faith we may need to pry open our fingers and open our arms to a surprising God..."
From "Turn My Mourning into Dancing" by Henri Nouwen, "Opening to a Surprising God," Page #37-39

I grew up in rural southern Idaho where life turned slowly and predictably. Pastoring in urban Seattle is fun and dangerous and mind-blowing because Jesus keeps showing up in all the wrong places and in the wrong faces. As a child it was pretty clear to me 'who was in and who was out'. As an adult, I have yet to find the person or space where Jesus is not already present laughing, loving and confronting.

I have seen greater living faith among those on the streets than in the pews. Some of the most loving examples of Jesus have come from persons with same-sex orientation. In the Native American communities, the Holy Spirit is revealed in both Christo-centric and nativist faith traditions.

Each time Jesus jumps past one of my lines defining who is in and who is outside this faith I have to redraw a new line, to make room, to allow the indiscretion, to make sense of it. Then Jesus walks past my new line. I gave up drawing lines. My fingers and hands have been pried open time and again. Uncomfortable? Yes. Fun? Yes!

One of the themes that emerges and re-emerges in these last weeks is just this. Who is in? Who is out? And so we find Jesus defending a Roman centurion, making room for disciples whom he did not commission, receiving a criminal dying on a cross, forgiving the sin of an adulterous woman...

What becomes very apparent to a student of the Word is just how apt the writers were thirty to fifty years later re-telling the story. They were artists at forming words, sentences, even entire books. They wrote creatively and consistently reflecting and then challenging the morays of their time. The order in which they placed events often had less to do with historical order as theological content or story-telling. They placed stories in their place for emphasis. They became good at surprising us with their Jesus stories.

Reflections on "God Surprises!"

Consider todays text about 'blessing the children' in Matthew 19: 13-15. Note where it is placed, sandwiched between a confrontation by the Pharisees over divorce and the frustration of the disciples with Jesus apparently conserving view of marriage and the Story of the Rich young ruler.

Note: Remember in the story (as imagined by Terry) "Gathering Storm" the emphasis is upon the liberal view held by the Sadducees over divorce; allowing it for almost any reason—challenging it, yet implying a gracious Moses.

Q: Why do you suppose the story about Jesus blessing children follows the teaching encounter with the Pharisees about divorce and the Disciples private questions with the lines Jesus drew?

Q: Were the disciples and Pharisees similar in each story? ...How so?

Q: Where would you have been in the story of the children: Playing or controlling? ...How so?

Consider how God keeps messing with your own faith. How God surprises you.

Turn your thoughts to prayer for yourself, your church or community.

Week-4: WEDNESDAY—MATTHEW 5: 43-45 & 19: 16-22 & JOHN 9:1-5

STORY 13—COMPLETED BY LOVE

The Pharisees and Scribes had left. The crowd had thinned, most concluding there would be no more teaching that day. Jeshua had spent the better part of the day playing with the children, blessing others and telling stories that their ears would enjoy. He was in the middle of a story about a farmer with two sons. Both were given instructions to work in their father's field. One, the younger who said at first that he would not go to the field as directed, felt bad, upon reflection and in the end, did. The elder brother who had declared his obedience, in word, failed to actually go to the field. "So which of these, the younger or older, do you think obeyed their papa?" Jesus inquired, looking intently into the faces of the thirty or so children gathered around him. A young girl, maybe seven or eight raised her hand in respect, but spoke out before Jeshua could pick her, her voice betraying her excitement. "The younger one." Then she looked down, aware of her indiscretion. Jeshua smiled. "That's right, the younger."

Suddenly the crowd near the front seemed to part like a giant wave of the sea. I was seated just behind the children, next to Matthew and glanced to my right to see what all the commotion was about. Typically, we disciples would have caught the approach of anyone to discern intent and if the timing for an intrusion were right. But Jeshua had pretty much scolded us as we had been doing just that earlier in the day when parents were bringing their children. "Let the children alone!" he had said to us, *"And do not hinder them* from coming to Me; *for the kingdom of heaven belongs to such as these"* (Matthew 19:14).

Matthew recognized the young man for whom the crowd showed respect. He leaned over. "His name is Jacob. His papa and mama suddenly fell ill, about four years ago and died, leaving him over his sister and in charge of a vast wealth." 'Evidently', I thought, 'Matthew knew the family and well, from his tax collection days.' Matthew continued to give background. "He is highly respected, as his papa was. He is good to his sister and family and his servants. He runs his papa's olive oil business well." Even the children, recognizing his apparent wealth, if not his person, made room. Jeshua seemed a bit oblivious, bringing yet another child to his lap for blessing or another story, perhaps. Jacob called out to Jesus, unafraid and with just a hint of arrogance, interrupting him. *"Teacher, what good thing shall I do that I may obtain eternal life?"* Jeshua placed his hand on the little girl in his lap as if to bless and closing his eyes, prayed. "Papa, hold this little one always, as I do now. Give her your heart and eyes to see the poor and meet their needs." With that he hugged her and motioned her back to her parents. They seemed delighted, though a little startled that their daughter was welcomed before this young man, a ruler in the synagogue at Capernaum. Looking up, Jesus responded to Jacob. I could not tell if he was slighted at the delay. *"Why are you asking Me about what is good? There is only One who is good.* You study the scriptures. In humility, meditate upon them and you will know what you should do." Jacob's face betrayed his thoughts. He was taken back at the Master's instruction to read the Torah, which was his habit and pleasure to read. 'Did he not know who he was? His position?' A smile slowly emerged, as the young man composed himself and took a few steps sideways, looking down, as if in contemplation. He tried again. "Good teacher. I read and often, the Torah. My heart remains, somehow incomplete."

Jesus' own face softened, as it does when someone's plight is felt in Jeshua as compassion. Looking intently into Jacob's face, he continued. "All right then." he began slowly. "You are a son of Israel. It is Yahweh's love that alone is good. ...but if you wish to enter into life, keep the commandments." Looking carefully, I noticed that Jacob's demeanor seemed to change. He no longer seemed concerned with appearance, only truth. Reaching out to one of the children near and gently touching his head, he looked directly at Jesus. "Master," he spoke, softly, with respect. "Which ones? The laws of Moses or of the Scribes and teachers of the law?"

Impressed with the young man's change of spirit and apparent learning, Jeshua slowly stood and engaged more deeply. *"You shall not commit murder; You shall not commit adultery; You shall not steal; You shall not bear false witness; Honor your father and mother..."* Jeshua hesitated, noting the sudden pain in his eyes at the mention of his papa and mama. Jeshua took a step or two forward toward him. No one around was talking. All eyes on this moment, obviously filled with eternal meaning. ".and," Jeshua added with some emphasis, *"You shall love your neighbor as yourself."* The young man said to Him, his eyes moistening. *"All these things I have kept;"* Now he looked down in obvious reflection and then up into Jesus eyes. "but, what am I still lacking?" Jeshua seemed deeply moved. He walked over to the young man and placing his hand on his shoulder continued. *"If you wish to be complete, go and sell your possessions and give to the poor, and you will have treasure in heaven; and come, follow Me"* (Italic selections from Matthew 19: 16-21).

I watched Jacob's face turn from hopefulness, to pain and finally a kind of loss or grief, all within a few seconds. Slowly and taking one last moment to glance down at Jesus hand on his shoulder. He placed his own hand over Jeshua's and then, saying nothing, turned and walked away from Jeshua's presence and back up the hill, in silence. His sadness was immediately felt by all who had watched and listened. I sat in complete shock and sorrow. Not since the time of our calling had I remembered my Master making such an impassioned plea for a son of Israel to join us, who were the chosen.

Once again, the crowd parted making room for this young ruler in Israel. For all in Israel new, great wealth was a sign of God's favor.

Reflections on "Completed by Love"

Again, I am always amazed at how God, together with his human writers weaves the elements of The Story…

Q: Why do you suppose the story about the rich young ruler is placed immediately following Jesus blessing the children and his encounters with the Pharisees about divorce? …What is Matthew's (and Mark's for that matter) purpose?

Q: Stated differently, is there a reason the focus on children is narrated between two stories about the difficulty of following?

Place yourself in these stories:

Q: Are you more likely to argue with Jesus, sit in his lap or seek to know why you are still lacking?

Q: What do you 'lack' in becoming complete?

Q: What would Jesus ask you to do or give up in order to complete your freedom to really be his disciple?

Pray for yourself… ask Jesus 'what you lack' if anything?

Week-4: THURSDAY—MATTHEW 5: 48 & 6: 19-21 & MARK 10: 23-31

STORY 14—WEALTH AND MISSION

As Jacob, the rich young ruler made his way up the hill, Jeshua's eyes seemed strangely alone. Quietly, almost in a whisper, he allowed his thoughts to find words. *"How hard it will be for those who are wealthy to enter the kingdom of God!"* (Mark 10:23b) Jesus walked a little distance up the hill and into the crowd of several hundred still present.

Lifting his voice, almost as a plea, he began his final message for the people this day. Dusk would soon be upon us. *"Children, how hard it is to enter the kingdom of God!"* (Mark 10: 24b) Then he began a series of kingdom stories. The crowd settled into his teaching. Suddenly, he stopped and took a sweeping gaze over the whole community nestled against the hill. "I tell you plainly," lifting his voice. "You will not see the Son of Man again until he has come into the Kingdom prepared from before time!" With that Jesus turned suddenly, walking south. Matthew bid his friend Malchius, goodbye. We followed in silence.

Jeshua took us south and further into the hill country, along the east side of the Sea. It was dark as we made camp and finally settled in around a bristling camp fire. I had said nothing to anyone in the last two hours. My heart was sifting through the events of this Sabbath day. In Capernaum and again at the seashore I had seen the rising hostility of the elders. A heavy fear awakened. 'What,' I wondered, 'did the Master mean in saying that the people of Capernaum would see Jesus again, only at the coming of his kingdom? Perhaps,' I allowed a little hope, 'betrayal by the elders would lead to this Kingdom of God.' One thing was certain, my feelings were trying to catch up with my thoughts. Money and power were not the signs of God's approval. Nor were sickness and poverty evidence of God's disapproval. ...so what will be important in Jeshua's reign?'

As usual Peter broke the silence and echoed what we were all wrestling with. "Lord, if that young man, as honest, sincere and successful as he apparently is, cannot enter your kingdom, who can?" "Simon," Jesus responded, emphasizing in the use of his old name, Peter's humanness. "Simon. Every son of Adam loves something or someone more than my Papa. Each of us must wrestle with ourselves to enter the Kingdom of my Papa." As he spoke he was stroking the fire for emphasis. "It is easier for a camel to kneel and crawl through the Eye of the Needle gate in Jerusalem than it is for a man with riches to enter the Kingdom."

Jeshua fell silent and looked around the fire to each of us, the flames were now dancing between us. Peter again responded. *"Jesus! We have left everything and followed You."* Jeshua turned to Peter and smiled, knowing that he did not get it. None of us did, really. "Peter, know this for certain. *No one who has left houses or brothers or sisters or mother or father or children or farms, for My sake and for the gospel's sake, will fail to receive a hundred times as much now in the present age, houses and brothers and sisters and mothers and children and farms, along with persecutions; and in the age to come, eternal life"* (Mark 10: 28-30).

With that the fire crackled. Silence again enveloped us as we struggled to take that in. 'Had I just heard the promise of a king to his loyal subjects?' My feelings were mixed. I wanted to avoid the fate to which Jesus seemed to be moving. And how I longed for eternal life. That alone would make my life complete, I knew. 'Did I really want houses and gold and honors bestowed upon me, as a king would?' My thoughts were soon exposed. Looking right at me, Jeshua said his last words before retiring. *"But many who are first will be last, and the last, first"* (Mark 10: 31).

Reflections on "Wealth and Mission"

Q: What motivates you, as you enter the mission of our Lord? ...Prestige, acceptance, love, or _____?

Q: What have you left, to follow?

Let your thoughts turn to prayer.

Week-4: FRIDAY—MATTHEW 5: 33-37 & 20: 1-16

My Thoughts 10—Promises, Promises

"Suddenly it can hit you how fleeting our existence is, how like water that we cannot hold in our hand. Recognizing this can fill us with sadness, since it makes us realize that something of us is dying all the time.

It may lead us to conclude that we should never expect much. It may make us forget that new possibilities almost always wait around the corner. …For those who have eyes to see and ears to hear, much in our fleeting lives is not passing but lasting, not dying but coming to life, not temporary but eternal. Amid the fragility of our lives, we have wonderful reason to hope."

From "Turn My Mourning into Dancing" by Henri Nouwen, "From Fatalism to Hope," Page #37-39

The previous story of the rich young ruler was scandalous precisely because it challenged the assumption of service and reward. If wealth doesn't demonstrate God's acceptance, what does? And so Matthew remembers well the struggle of Jesus disciples: If those who have positions of trust and who are blessed by God can't get into the eternal inheritance, because of their great money, what of the poor? Peter personalizes it: If we who have left all to follow you cannot count on reward, who can?

Now, Matthew was a tax collector. He understood the value of money and the relation of work, of effort and reward. It is no accident that he places the story Jesus told of the workers who worked a full day and those who came late to the party (uh, job) receiving the same wages (Matt 20: 1-16) and immediately after the encounter with the rich young ruler. Peter's emphatic question, 'Who then can be saved?' has been trumped… everyone gets the same reward? How unfair! It's as if he is emphasizing the scandalous nature of Jesus theology of reward. No union boss would ever want Jesus in charge of the negotiations.

And so, Matthew tempers it just a bit. He does the math and remembers Jesus saying that those who have left family, houses and businesses will in the renewal of all things receive a hundred-fold back, plus eternal life. Problem solved.

Not really. C.S. Lewis notes that to our modern (post-modern) ears the idea of reward and mission itself feels wrong; like a warrior who markets himself or herself out to a fight rather than battling for a purpose worth giving up even life itself for. But the New Testament is full of reward theology without shame. To be sure most of it is the immediate or delayed result of living into the creativity and love of God in a universe of God's creation. So the reward and the mission are simply part of each other like the taste of apple pie alamode fresh from an oven and the hands that formed the tender crust and picked the apples and smothered it all in ice-cream. It melts in our mouth.

Lewis goes onto suggest that not only is the reward to be part of the motive but that the failure to entertain reward/punishment leaves us with the problem of 'wanting too little' and thus missing out on the new world God is creating. He suggests we are like children making mud pies in the middle of a tenant housing project when God has promised nothing short of Disneyland.

And so we come full circle. The important thing is just getting in on the surprises of God's love and life among us.

Whether we come early or late will not matter because the pie tastes so good that all thought of 'justice or fairness' is lost in the pleasure of the reward.

Reflections on "Promises, Promises"

Q: With what reward will you be satisfied?

Consider the nature of reward-punishment, gifting and refusal of gift... Reflect and listen:

Week-4: SATURDAY—MATTHEW 5: 11-12 & MARK 10: 32-34

STORY 15—DESTINY

"John, wake up!" It took a while. I had slept and deeply, in my own bed at Bethsaida. Jeshua and the twelve had stayed with my papa and mother as well. I felt Peter's hand shake me. For a moment I felt as if I was a little boy at home with my papa wakening me for a day on the lake, fishing. "John, hurry! Jeshua's left, with Judas Iscariot." At the mention of Jeshua's name I shook off my dreamy state and came to. "Gone? Where? With Judas!?" I replied. Peter pointed down the sea shore. "That way, toward Jerusalem, by way of the eastern plains along Galilee." Nothing more need be said. I understood his anxiety. All of us did. Over the next ten minutes the twelve gathered our belongings and moved south to catch up with the Master. Peter, as always, broke our silent urgency. "Well, it's about time." He laughed. "To Jerusalem for glory then..." He paused. "or death."

At the south end of the lake, beyond Hippos, the road comes to a crossroads. We stopped and waited, not knowing what to do. Peter and James went down to the shore to do some fishing. Andrew and I walked up into the hills. Since our days with the Baptist the desert had an attraction and the hills south and east of Galilee reminded us of the old days with the Baptist in similar terrain. Andrew stopped along a stream and sat down, as if to rest. I soon realized that it was his spirit that needed rest. We sat in silence for the better part of an hour until Andrew at last spoke. I wasn't sure if he was speaking to me or the wind. "How will it all end?" He began. "In death, as it was for the Baptist or..." He stopped. I think, not knowing how to frame what success would feel like. Jeshua was unlike any other leader or Rabbi, for that matter. "It will end well, Andrew!" We turned around. We had been facing the stream, oblivious to the approach of Jesus and the ten who were now with him. Stepping forward and reaching his hand out to Andrew's shoulder, Jesus continued. "It will end well, but..." he paused as the other ten gathered in around us. Jeshua's voice was soft, not reflective, more purposeful. "It will not feel well, but will end well. *We are going up to Jerusalem and the Son of Man will be betrayed to the chief priests and teachers of the law. They will condemn him to death and will hand him over to the Gentiles, who will mock him and spit on him, flog him and kill him."* Jesus had been moving around the circle placing his hands on each of our shoulders. When he came back to me, still seated by Andrew, though turning around into the circle, he sat down. Opening his arms wide and then raising them to the heavens, he finished. *"Three days later he will rise"* (Matthew 10: 32-34). We all stood and sat motionless for what seemed a very long time. Slowly I turned away and back to the creek. Dusk was now upon us. My thoughts betrayed my doubts. 'Of course he will rise, as will the Baptist at that last day.' I failed to see how that is ending well.

Reflections on "Destiny"

Q: What were your initial expectations when you first met Jesus? ...What did you expect from life, from Jesus, from yourself?

Q: Are you surprised? ...Disappointed? ...How so?

Reflect on the expectations you first had and the life and rhythms you now enjoy with Jesus... Turn it to prayer; toward thanksgiving or confession:

Week-4: SUNDAY— MATTHEW 5: 13 & LUKE 9: 51-55 & LUKE 12: 49-56 & JOHN 14: 25-27 & GALATIANS 2: 1-16 & 3: 26-28

STORY 16—LAST CHANCE

The next morning, we again turned south towards Jericho. When we came to the cross roads, near Beth Shean, Jeshua surprised us. He had steadily been moving toward Jerusalem, the place of his predicted suffering and following, we had hoped, the beginning of his rule as Messiah. At this cross roads we could continue south toward Jericho and then up and over the mountains, past Bethany and into Jerusalem. Or, if we wished we could turn west again before turning south and into the hill country of the Samaritans. Jews traveling from the north of the Sea of Galilee would often move along the Jordan river, as we had, to avoid the Samaritan villages.

Four hundred years of arguing about what a real Jew looked like had left a cultural, religious and ethnic gulf between Samaritans and Judeans and Galileans. The argument was centered upon weather the Temple in Jerusalem and the spiritual elders there occupied Moses seat or if, as the Samaritans claimed, there were many holy places in Israel, acceptable to the worship of Yahweh. I had been raised to think of Samaritans as half breeds and spiritual bastards who had forsaken Yahweh to worship many gods. In truth, I despised Samaritans. Jesus didn't. In the months before he had sent 70 disciples into Galilee and Samaria. He had often directed us through Samaritan villages and treated individual Samaritans as daughters and sons of Moses.

And now, instead of turning toward Jerusalem in preparation for the coming festival of Passover, he once again looked west and south to those Jeshua called, our cousins. So we found a place near ancient Beth Shean, now called Scythopolis and camped. Peter fished for the evening's meal. Judas went into the district capital nearby for provisions. Andrew, James, Bartholomew, Thomas, Judas the son of Alpheus and I were sent by Jesus up and into Samaria to make preparations for one last and brief mission in Samaria before Passover. Jesus prayed.

The six of us had returned by mid-evening of the next day to rendezvous and compare notes. The others had reported little response which had surprised all of us, given the investment of the seventy sent out months earlier. 'Perhaps,' I thought to myself, 'their previous reports of success were overstated,' smiling at the thought of the twelve's superior training and skill. Judas the son of Alpheus and I reported something more akin to hostility. We were anxious to let Jesus know of our experience and set out for camp.

Arriving, we found Jesus, the other six and some village elders, apparently Pharisees, laughing and enjoying a rather heated debate. Jeshua's voice was raised, as if in response and to a previous part of the discussion. *"When you see a cloud rising in the west, immediately you say, 'It's going to rain,' and it does. And when the south wind blows, you say, 'It's going to be hot,' and it is. Hypocrites!"* I noticed that Jeshua's voice and body did not betray anger but good hearted bantering. He continued. *"You know how to interpret the appearance of the earth and the sky. How is it that you don't know how to interpret this present time?"* (Luke 12: 54-56)

Just then Jeshua saw the six of us approaching. He waved us in and without concern for appearance, invited us to report the day's response from Samaritan villages. I was last to speak. I had noticed how the Pharisees had turned from a light hearted and joyous debate to silence and concern as they discovered the Master's intent to minister among Samaritan villages. Jeshua simply bowed his head,

Who Am I?

obviously saddened. At the end of James report there was silence. Finally, Jeshua looked up, his eyes hopeful of something better. "And John," he asked. "What was the response to you and Judas, son of Alpheus?"

"Master," I began slowly. "We sought out the elders at the gate. We informed them of your desire to come. I," hesitating, "I, uh, had emphasized that you were on your way to Jerusalem from Capernaum and were anxious to visit before the festival." Jesus frowned, knowing the indiscretion I had shown—as most Samaritans felt the festival gatherings in Jerusalem an insult to their own cultural heritage. "They asked where we were camped. I told them. They talked among themselves and suggested that if you were truly interested in their wellbeing you might have come yourself and camped in the heart of Samaria, rather than on the border keeping your options for a Jordanian route open." Jesus simply nodded. "Master," I continued, pleading as I had with the elders of the village. "Master, I explained your heart as open and how we had often traveled through Samaria." I then observed the Pharisees reaction to news of the Master's openness to Samaritans and how similar it appeared to the Samaritans reaction to us. I paused briefly and continued. "All they could say was that following your time in Jerusalem, 'let him come to Sychar and sacrifice with us. Let's see how accepting he is of our invitation!' And with that, Master, they stood, took off their sandals, shook out their robes and turned to walk away with no further word." I bristled in anger as I remembered the feeling of absolute rejection by the elders of this village. I could see the dark stir of emotion in all who listened. Without thinking I added. *"Lord, do want us to call fire down from heaven to destroy them?"* (Luke 9: 54b)

I looked around the fire. All the eyes stared first at me and then turned to see Jeshua's response. On each face was a myriad of feelings. Anger, surprise and a sense of audacity, at the suggestion we had such power. Silence followed. No one dare speak. Finally, Jesus looked up. "John, son of thunder," He began, his own eyes betraying an angry sadness. "What do you think? Is this why I have come into the world? To inflame the hatred of brother for brother?" With that he stood and turned his back sideways to us, hands folded across his lower stomach, in apparent thought. Awkwardly, the six of us joined the others around the fire, awaiting our Master's next response.

Reflections on "Last Chance"

Jesus prayer in John 17: 20-23 reflects the truth that the world will believe in Jesus only when the Church is One with the Trinity of God and each other.

Q: Will it ever be? …Can love truly trump power and prejudice?

Q: What do we do with those faiths that share many of our tenants, but are not historically Christian? …Do we begin with them as believers?

Your reflections: Then, pray for those communities of faith that are, perhaps, Pre-Christian.

Who Am I?

5 Comfort and Loss
...The Approaching Sorrow amid Signs of Hope

INVOCATION:

LORD, WE LIFT UP OUR EYES TO THE HILLS- THE HILLS WHERE THE FLOODS GATHER AND THE EARTH SHAKES. WHERE, O LORD, CAN WE FIND HELP WHEN SURROUNDED BY BEAUTY THAT IN A MOMENT BECOMES DISASTER AND REMINDS US WE ARE NOTHING? WE KNOW. OUR HELP COMES FROM THE LORD, THE MAKER OF HEAVEN AND EARTH.

EVEN WHEN WALKING ALONG A MOUNTAIN PRECIPICE YOU WILL NOT LET US STUMBLE AND FALL TO OUR DEATH. ALWAYS, AT NIGHT AND IN THE DAY YOU ARE AWAKE WITH CONCERN FOR OUR PATH. THANK YOU, LORD.

YOU, WHO KEEPS WATCH OVER ISRAEL, NEVER TIRES AND NEVER SLEEPS. THE LORD WATCHES OVER US—THE LORD IS OUR SHADE FROM THE SCORCHING SUN. AND THE MOON'S LIGHT GIVES LIGHT ON THE DARKEST EVENING. THE LORD WILL KEEP US FROM EVERY HARM—HE WATCHES OVER OUR LIVES.

THE LORD WATCHES OVER OUR COMING AND GOING, NOW AND FOREVER. AMEN

ADAPTED FROM PSALM 121

PSALM OF THE WEEK: PSALM 131

QUOTE OF THE WEEK: WHAT MIGHT GOD BE DOING HERE?
FROM "TURN MY MOURNING INTO DANCING" BY HENRI NOUWEN, PG #56.

DAILY SCRIPTURES:

MONDAY—MATTHEW 5: 43-48 & LUKE 10: 25-37

TUESDAY—MATTHEW 7: 24-27 & 18: 15-20

WEDNESDAY—MATTHEW 7: 28-29 & LUKE 9: 57-62 & JOHN 15: 13-17

THURSDAY—MATTHEW 7:12 & 11: 25-30 & LUKE 10: 1-24

FRIDAY—MATTHEW 7: 15-20 & 20: 20-24

Saturday—Matthew 7: 21-23 & John 11: 1-16

SUNDAY—MATTHEW 6: 14-15 & MARK 10: 41-45 & PHILIPPIANS 2: 1-18 & 4: 1-13

Real Time and Clock Time
From
Turn My Mourning Into Dancing
by Henri Nouwen
Page #55

As still not completely converted people we immerse ourselves in clock time. Time becomes a means to an end, not moments in which to enjoy God or pay attention to others. And we end up believing that the real thing is always still to come. Time for celebrating or praying or dreaming gets squeezed out. No wonder we get fatigued and deflated! No wonder we sometimes feel helpless or impoverished in our experience of time.

But the gospel speaks of "full" time. What we are seeking is already here. The contemplative Thomas Merton once wrote, "The Bible is concerned with time's fullness, the time for an event to happen, the time for an emotion to be felt, the time for a harvest or for the celebration of a harvest." We begin to see history not as a collection of events interrupting what we "must" get done. We see time in light of faith in the God of history. We see how events of this year are not just a series of incidents and accidents, happy or unhappy, but the molding hands of God, who wants us to grow and mature.

Week-5: MONDAY— MATTHEW 5: 43-48 & LUKE 10: 25-37
Story 17—Prejudice

Jesus just stood there, not five feet from the fire. He now stood sideways to those of us gathered around the fire. His arms remained folded and his spirit seemed deflated as he stood motionless and gazing into the night.

None of us spoke. Not even the Pharisees and scribes gathered with us, from Scythopolis. My suggestion that judgment come to the Samaritan villages that had rejected our invitation to visit them had been thoroughly rebuked by Jesus.

Finally, one of the scribes, an expert in the law spoke up, trying to continue the pleasant debate that was ensuing when the six of us returned from Samaria. *"Teacher,"* he asked, *"what must I do to inherit eternal life?"* He had stood to capture Jesus attention and command authority.

Slowly Jesus gaze relented and he turned toward the scribe, keeping his arms folded but relaxing and with a bit of a smile on his face, knowing the intent. *"What is written in the Law?"* he replied. *"How do you read it?"* The scribe looked down thoughtfully, taking the question seriously. *He answered: "'Love the Lord your God with all your heart and with all your soul and with all your strength and with all your mind'; and,"* he added *letting both hands extend in front of him for emphases. "Love your neighbor as yourself.'"* Jeshua looked into the scribe's eyes in silence. I think He knew he was standing before a thoughtful and devout follower of his papa. Finally, Jeshua walked over and placed one hand upon the scribe's shoulder before continuing. *"You have answered correctly… Do this and you will live"* (from Luke 10: 25-28).

Another of the Pharisees, perhaps a little uncomfortable at the implications of his friend's theology and in light of the previous discussions about Samaritans tried to define the term neighbor. He looked up and without much thought, it appeared, asked Jeshua. *"And who is my neighbor?"*

Jeshua simply began to walk around the outer circle of those gathered. After a few seconds he responded. *"A man was going down from Jerusalem to Jericho when he fell into the hands of robbers."* All of us knew that journey, high in the mountains over a narrow and dangerous path, in places. Robbers abounded on it, for there was no escape. My thoughts quickly returned to the story Jeshua was telling. *"They stripped him of his clothes, beat him and went away, leaving him half dead. A priest happened to be going down the same road, and when he saw the man, he passed by on the other side. So too a Levite, when he came to the place and saw him, passed by on the other side. But a Samaritan…"* Jesus paused for a moment. I looked around trying to observe the response of the Pharisees and scribes as Jesus spoke. I had not heard this story but knew it would come to a revealing end. Jeshua never used such personal illustrations unless he was either confronting enemies or revealing an important truth. Our guests sat in cold silence, revealing nothing. All that is, except the Pharisee who had quoted the Shema and added the command to love your neighbor. His head was bowed, as in deep thought. Jeshua continued, "A Samaritan, *as he traveled, came where the man was; and when he saw him, he took pity on Him. He went to him and bandaged his wounds, pouring on oil and wine. Then he put the man on his own donkey, took him to an inn and took care of him."* Jesus stopped walking and turned into the circle and sat down before continuing. *"The next day he took out* two silver coins *and gave them to the innkeeper. 'Look after him,' he said, 'and when I return, I will reimburse you for any extra expense you may have.'"* Jesus looked around the fire at each of us, with care, before continuing. *"Which of these three do you think was a neighbor to the man who fell into the hands of robbers?"* Without pause, the scribe who had initiated the discussion looked up from staring into the fire and with a kind of awe spoke. *"The one who had mercy on him."* Jesus, looking back at the scribe smiled. *"Go and do likewise"* (Luke 10: 29-37).

The Pharisee who had wanted to narrow the definition of neighbor simply grunted and stood. He then gave appreciation to all for an interesting evening and left. The other scribes and Pharisees followed him. All but the scribe who had asked, "What must I do to inherit eternal life?" He stayed and talked with Jesus late into the evening.

Reflections on "Prejudice"

Q: What prejudices have you noticed in yourself. …Do they trouble you?

Q: Who are your neighbors? …Who surrounds your life? …Do you know them? …Do you care to know them?

Week-5: TUESDAY—MATTHEW 7: 24-27 & 18: 15-20
My Thoughts 11—Back to our Future

"We first look backward to see how our lives' seemingly unrelated events have brought us to where we are... Sorting through memories means holding painful recollections in a certain way...

Memory also reminds us of the faithfulness of God in the hard places and joyous moments. It lets us see how God has brought good from even the impossible situations. Remembering in this way allows us to live in the present...

Memory, therefore, has much to do with the future. Without memory there is no expectation. Those who have little memory have little to expect. Memory anchors us in the past and then makes us present here and now."

"Turn My Mourning Into Dancing" by Henri Nouwen, "Reading Life Backward." Page #59-60

A stream of thoughts from my own Journal Dated May 31, 2010 ...Trinity Sunday:

I used to think that God was happy or sad according to weather I pleased or angered him. Then for a season in my life, I thought that maybe God is always happy with me without regard to my behavior or feelings in a given moment.

The truth is God is neither so dependent upon my joy or sorrow, my goodness or badness. The Father truly is free to love and live, laugh and cry according to the joy or sorrow the Father shares with the Son and the Spirit and their experience of the six billion of my fellow creatures who live inside the dance of the stars and galaxies.

Within my Savior's heart and the Spirit and the Father who share in his experiences and feelings is my own experience, my wounds and needs. No less than the dust of the stars I can effect and affect my God's heart.

I have come to see that the Trinity of God is at times angry, happy, pleased, saddened as The Father—Son—Spirit enter into even my experience. God is moved by me. What a thought! But it is the movement, the rhythm of love;

Beating,

   Longing,

      Hoping,

         Dreaming me ever closer to the other six billion and to the wonder of galaxies dancing.

(Note: adapted from my journal)

Reflections on "Back to our Future"

In this quickly written stream of thoughts Terry has tried to balance the following:

- God's freedom to be a full Being, capable of all emotion, passionate in feeling, and;
- God's absolute love, and;
- God's otherness as a Being beyond our own experience and;

> Love's ability to care about and focus upon all of creation, including each person, animal and rock in creation.

Your Reflections: Take a moment and reflect, then, turn it to a prayer.

Week-5: WEDNESDAY—Matthew 7: 28-29 & Luke 9: 57-62 & John 15: 13-17

Story 18—The Call

We were not far from Jericho and were moving further south along the Jordan. The crowds along the route were beginning to increase as always happened within a week or two of Passover and the festival in Jerusalem. From all over Judea and Galilee one could hear the psalms of assent being sung by small groups of travelers on their way to Jerusalem. My mama and papa, together with Jeshua's mama and sister had joined us the night before. Mama, bless her soul, had again reminded me to watch closely Jeshua's actions, believing that he would now come into his kingdom in Jerusalem. "Listen to your mama!" She had scolded, thinking I was not paying enough attention. It was about the first watch of the night. "Your brother James," she continued, "will be an excellent administrator for Jesus!" I nodded, recognizing his role as the chief administrator in my papa's fishing business, before Jesus.

The next day Judas, son of Alpheus was leading the men of our little band in Psalm 122. *"I rejoiced with those who said to me, 'Let us go to the house of the LORD.'"* Picking up her queue, mama, together with Mary, her sister and the other women in our band responded. *"Our feet are standing in your gates, O Jerusalem."* It all seemed familiar and comforting, being caught up inside these yearly rituals which formed the heart and faith of Israel.

Suddenly, a young man, probably my age, from somewhere in the front of our group, stopped and turned. Evidently the excitement of the approaching festival and the throngs of

Israel's children making their pilgrimage overwhelmed him. He, together with a handful of his friends looked intently upon my Master. Noticing, Jeshua stopped, acknowledging their apparent interest. My mama stopped her singing and standing next to Jeshua took in the unfolding scene.

Then, without further invitation, this young man spoke up. *"I will follow you wherever you go."* Jesus smiled, but his answer betrayed his skepticism. *"Foxes have dens and birds of the air have nests, but the Son of Man has no place to lay his dead."* My thoughts quickly turned to the rich young ruler who had approached Jesus a few days earlier, his arrogance exposed. But then Jesus took me by surprise. Looking at the second man, much older than the first, Jeshua simply said. *"Follow me"* (Luke 9: 57-59a). I was astonished. Not since the calling of my cousin, Peter had I seen such a simple and direct invitation to follow and join the twelve.

'What is it he sees in this middle aged man?' I thought. Obviously he was a devout pilgrim, but so were the thousands who were making the trip. "Lord," the man replied. "My father is aged and nearing his time of rest. Allow me to go and bury him first. Then I will come and finding you, gladly follow!" Jesus simply stood still, studying his face. Slowly, he approached this man. "Tell me," he began. "What is your name?" "David," the man replied. His eyes, younger than his apparent age, sparkled in the sun's light. "David," Jesus replied. "There is time for burial. Those who are dead in spirit will still take care of those who are dead in body." And placing his hands on both shoulders, as though imploring, Jesus continued. "But you, go and proclaim the Kingdom of God." To which the man simply nodded agreement. I knew I was witnessing a covenant between them.

The third man, whose age appeared to be older than me, but much younger than David, interrupted the sacred inside this moment, abruptly. *"I will follow you, Lord; but first let me go back and say good bye to my family."* Almost annoyed, Jesus turned his head to him and replied. *"No one who puts his hand to the plow and looks back is fit for service in the kingdom of God"* (Luke 9: 61-62). Rebuked, the man simply turned and left.

Again my thoughts turned to the rich young ruler, Jacob, from Capernaum. 'Who then,' I thought to myself, 'can make it? What is the criterion by which one man is given mercy and another is refused?' Jesus, simply turned to me and watching my eyes responded. "John, no one comes to me, unless drawn by My Papa, who sees all."

Reflections on "The Call"

As you reflect on our text: John 15: 13-17

Q: What is the basis of acceptance or rejection by God? ...Is it passion or compassion?

Q: What has priority in your life? ...Mission or _____ ?

Your Reflections:

Week-5: THURSDAY—MATTHEW 7:12 & 11: 25-30 & LUKE 10: 1-24

MY THOUGHTS 12—DOWN AND DIRTY

"If someone asked you if you were compassionate, you might readily say yes. Or at least, 'I believe so.' But pause to examine the word compassion and answering gets more complicated. For the word comes from roots that mean literally to 'suffer with'; to show compassion means sharing in the suffering 'passion' of another. Compassion understood in this way asks more from us than a mere stirring of pity or a sympathetic word...

In so many encounters we try to look away from the pain. We try to help our friends quickly process grief. We hastily look for ways to bring cheer to a child or ailing aunt. All the while, however, we act less out of genuine 'suffering with' and more out of our need to stand back from the discomfort we fear we might feel. We secretly, restlessly want to move from the place where it hurts. Our evasions do not help others, To live with compassion means to enter others' dark moments. It is to walk into places of pain, not to flinch or look away when another agonizes."

From "My Mourning Into Dancing" by Henri Nouwen in "Manipulation to Love" Page #67-70

Several times over the course of these weeks we will see moments when Jesus discusses the approaching pain; most powerfully in the garden when he invites his protégés to stay up with him and pray. They slept. In each moment the disciples turn away from pain and back into their own imagined outcome of their narrative, 'success'...

When approached by a leper, Jesus reached out and touched, finding common humanity. When presented with a triumphal entry he fully engaged but with a sorrow that understood his breaking heart.

We are creatures of image...created in the image of Three who share a communion of love so powerful that they are in fact One in actualized essence. So when Jesus was on the cross, the Father and Spirit fully participated as they do even today as Jesus continues to express before the Father the aching empty spaces of the human heart as uncovered by the Spirit that groans within each and between all of us (ref: Romans 8: 26,27).

We who are Imago Deo, created in God's image and are called to increasingly enter into God's likeness are a trinity as well (Body, Soul and Spirit). So much human pain is simply the result of living one, perhaps two dimensional lives instead of the inter-penetrating, inter-actualizing of our body expressing soulfulness because we are spiritually connected with one another.

Nowhere is this more apparent than in our sexuality. We seek at best to express a soul filled love and affection in caresses, kisses and delighted exploration; but in a no strings attached kind of way. It doesn't work and ultimately we are lost to one dimensional addiction to our bodies imagining as a result. Within the sacrament that marriage is to be God desires to co-create in a communal commitment that would allow the highest expression of our sensuality that is expressive of joy, creativity, affection (soul).

Because of the tremendous gap between the Image of God (potential) and the un-likeness (likeness marred) we humans feel, the pain of empty longing is always present in us; Sensual longings drawn from the chasm of our own intuition of what we know should be possible and our continual choice to addict to the apple in our eye instead of a garden of delights if only we will walk inside God's good vision. The pain is real.

What we are called to give the world is 'reverence'… acceptance of the broken spaces in ourselves and others so that our fellowship, the Eucharist communion is an invitation of fellow humans becoming—(straight-gay-married-unmarried) but who are, as we all are, responding to the offer of Holy Love, of Communion with the only source of our healing; the Trinity of God present to us.

But instead of this 'reverence' for people as they/we are, we put up walls or quick fix remedies that say in one way or another…'go, get your act together and them come and join us at the table'. That is not the Jesus model who with the woman caught in adultery simply offered acceptance and gave a new direction toward wholeness… 'Go and sin no more'…

Even on the approaching last evening we will see Jesus reaching out to Judas; placing him in the position of honor, to his left and offering the Eucharist, advising that if he has to do it, get it done... get the pain over with and finally in the garden of betrayal asking him, "Judas, really, with a kiss?" It is the power of one who did not turn away from pain but embraced his own and others.

Reflections on "Down and Dirty"

In Matthew 11: 25-30 Jesus invites all of into a relationship where he, the eternal God will reverence us… will not put on us a religious tight belt, ill-fitting and uncomfortable…

Q: What do you think of Terry's suggestion that Jesus invitation (now in the Eucharist) is open to everyone who seeks?

Q: Have you ever really entered this place of 'peace', of acceptance, of rest? ...How so? ...Why not?

Q: How can you give reverence, if you do not receive it for yourself?

Take a moment and reflect, then, turn it to a prayer.

Week-5: FRIDAY—MATTHEW 7: 15-20 & 20: 20-24

STORY 19—GRAB FOR POWER

There is something magical about Jericho. The ancient story of her fall before Joshua's trumpets still echoed in our hearts. More recently, during the Maccabean rebellion Jericho had become the center of political activity for all who wanted freedom. To this day, there was a strong group of zealots in this city who plotted the over throw of Rome and waited only for the coming of Israel's Messiah, to join the struggle.

Jericho was the historic center for the production of palm branches. During the time of Maccabean rule and Judah's freedom from Grecian rule these branches became symbol of Judea's freedom from foreign domination. When we came into the Jericho we would buy a hundred or more so that we could scatter them along the road as we entered Jerusalem as a sign of the Messiah's coming. Most of those coming south from Galilee for the festival would do the same. Jerusalem would grow from a city of 50,000 to about 250,000 overnight. And the Romans would look on to manage the potential explosion of patriotic feeling, being helpless to forbid this public display of pride, waved in their faces. It would be an awesome moment. 'Who knows,' I thought to myself, 'maybe we will scatter the palm branches before Jeshua, if he allows.' Hurriedly, I corrected myself. 'Never would Jesus allow such a thing. Too bad.'

Just then my mama grabbed my tunic and pulled me to the side with James. Jesus had stopped for a rest. We couldn't have been more than two miles from Jericho. Perhaps it was the anticipation of entering Jericho or maybe the encounter with wanna be disciples that triggered her timing. Mama went over to Jeshua, who was seated against a rock, alone. Only Judas Iscariot was near enough to hear. How I wished he were not present. But mama, unaware of the inner workings of our little band was oblivious. She approached Jeshua and knelt down as one does before a king. She motioned us to do the same. James and I just looked at each other and as casually as possible knelt. I went to one knee hoping it would appear as nothing to the others and still seem reverent enough for my mama. James went down on all two. We glanced at each other and then I looked over to Judas. He had a quizzical look on his face and our behavior clearly peaked his interest. 'Great!' I thought. Jeshua simply looked up, took the view in and smiling addressed mama. *"What is it you want?" he asked.* (Matthew 20: 21a) Without hesitation and in clear, overly loud language, she began. "Master, my Lord," she stumbled, not sure of how to address her nephew for such an important issue. "As you know, my son James, your cousin, had been in charge of all the business affairs of Zebedee's business, before," she again was a little hesitant. "That is, before you had need of him." 'Oh brother,' I thought to myself. 'This is not going to be a good thing.' Jesus simply nodded agreement. Mama was now on a roll and was not to be stopped. "Good Master," she continued. "He was skilled in all of his relations and decisions. Our business prosperity is due his diligence, in no small measure." Jesus now knew what was coming, I think. His smile seemed a little more forced. I noticed that Judas was not smiling at all.

Mama simply continued, unaware of the changes in Jeshua's demeanor or the damage she was doing our reputation with the others. *"Grant that one of these two sons of mine may sit at your right hand and the other at your left* when you come into your kingdom. If I may be so bold," she continued, as though she had not been bold as yet. "May I suggest James for the right, as your chief minister and John, your trusted friend on your left as your chief counselor. You, of course, already know of his wisdom." (Matthew 20: 21b)

My heart sank within me. I wanted to look down and away. James seemed to be enjoying the whole thing, though I could not imagine why. Finally, mama closed her mouth, her eyes wide with anticipation of Jeshua's response. To his credit, Jesus smile broadened. For a moment I thought he might laugh and treat it as a kind of joke. 'Please, by all that is holy in Jerusalem,' my thoughts raced. 'May he do just that.' With a quiet grace, Jeshua reached out to mama and touched her hand and then looking into her eyes and reaching for her face with both of his hands and cupping her as one does a fragile creature, he began. *"You don't know what you're asking,* Salome." 'That was an understatement!' I thought. Then he asked her and us. *"Can you drink the cup I am going to drink?"* (Matthew 20: 22) James who had been looking down in a kind of humility raised his eyes to Jesus and nodded sincerely his affirmation. Mama simply said "yes", without so much as blinking. Glancing in Judas Iscariot's direction I responded, quietly but with confidence.

Jeshua was asking us as a bridegroom would his bride at the moment of engagement. In offering the cup of wine, a groom was saying to his beloved, 'all that I am or ever will be, I give to you.' And the betrothed could in that moment accept or reject. Acceptance of the cup was an act of full surrender to the lover of her soul. I knew now, that the net was spun. There was no turning back. For good or ill, mama had forced Jeshua's heart. "We can," was all I said.

Jesus response surprised me, though. *"You will indeed drink from my cup."* A feeling of great love overcame me in an instant. Never had I realized how much I longed for Jeshua's acceptance, for his love. Then, laying back once again against the rock he continued, but in a saddened voice. "The cup, you will drink, yes, *but to sit at my right or left is not for me to grant."* Mama's body seemed to sink with Jeshua's voice. Jeshua finished his thought. *"These places belong to those for whom they have been prepared by my Father"* (Matthew 20: 23). With that Jesus closed his eyes to rest. Judas, quietly but quickly moved away and toward the other ten, his body language clearly revealing something akin to rage. Mama, slowly, even awkwardly backed away, until it was comfortable to stand and go find Zebedee. I stared at James who looked deflated. I knew it had not ended here.

Reflections on "Grab for Power"

Consider this scene and how it would impact the disciple's relations in this vital last two weeks.

Q: Have you ever or are you now confusing your agenda with Gods?

Q: Where are some modern Jericho's? ...that is: Places where faith and nationalism merge to form a hybrid that, when fully developed becomes a perverted form of the gospel?

Pray and ask that God will walk with the church today as Jesus did in Jericho, defining the real issues facing us and our world.

Week-5: SATURDAY—MATTHEW 7: 21-23 & JOHN 11: 1-16
MY THOUGHTS 13—DISAPPOINTMENTS

"...for all the insights of popularized psychology, all the programs on relationships, all the seminars and conferences on healthy relationships, we still often are not happy. And because of our culture's emphasis on psychology and interpersonal relationships, we import a consumer mentality to our intimacies. We expect more of our friends and partners than they can (or want to) give. A fair amount of our suffering comes from our loneliness, a loneliness intensified by our high needs..."

From "Turn My Mourning Into Dancing" by Henri Nouwen in "Why Others Disappoint" Page #70-71

Albert Ellis in a 'Rational Guide to Emotive Therapy' argues persuasively that it is not any event which creates our feeling responses, but our interpretation of those events... He illustrates. That we think **A (event)** = **C (emotions)** when, in fact, our emotions are actually the result of a rational process **B (what we tell ourselves about an event** that produces in us emotional responses.

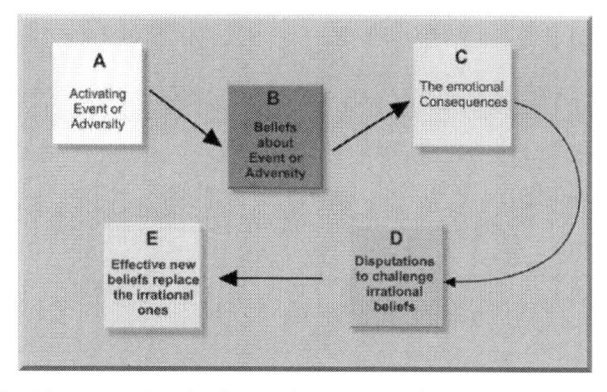

```
    A                          C
Activating                The emotional
Event or        B         Consequences
Adversity     Beliefs
              about
              Event or
              Adversity

    E                          D
Effective new           Disputations
beliefs replace   ←     to challenge
the irrational          irrational
    ones                  beliefs
```

His therapy technique is not to deny the self-messages but to consider them and ask if they are rational (an appropriate response) to what just happened. His view is that in most cases we 'awfulize' (his word) events; thinking at B (what we tell ourselves) in terms of adjectives and outcomes that are not usually rational… It is our words, our 'awfulizing' of past and present events that lead us into depressive prisons, not the event itself.

Reflections on "Disappointments"

Q: Have you ever wrestled with a depression rooted, in your perception (what you tell yourself), of another's disappointing response to your needs? …How so?

Q: Looking back were your own expectations of another's ability to love you exaggerated? …manipulative?

In John 11: 1-16 we see Jesus responding rationally and with great freedom to perceived loss… even as later, in response to Mary, he will weep. Jesus demonstrates a remarkable freedom from interpersonal expectations.

Your thoughts: Take a moment and reflect, then, turn it to a prayer for wisdom in the midst of real pain.

Week-5: SUNDAY—MATTHEW 6: 14-15 & MARK 10: 41-45 & PHILIPPIANS 2: 1-18 & 4: 1-13

STORY 20—UNRESOLVED CONFLICT

We had just broken camp and were moving into Jericho itself. I was traveling behind everyone else and walking next to Jesus. Judas Iscariot, noticing a beggar beside the road remarks, loud enough for all to hear. "Tell me, James, when you are the prime minister, will you still give alms to the poor or send your servant to complete this humble task?" James who was walking just ahead turned around and glanced in my direction, his face turning red in rage or embarrassment. I could not tell. It was Jesus response that surprised me.

"Judas!" Jesus shouted. "Come here, please." And taking two drachmas from his own coin purse, he instructed him to go and give the alms to the beggar. Judas was visibly angry. I only smiled, feeling justified. Then Jesus called the rest of us together. We gathered around. I was not sure where this was all heading. The last to enter our little circle was Judas, now humbled.

Jesus words were sharp and began as a rebuke. *"You know that those who are regarded as rulers of the Gentiles lord it over them, and their high officials exercise authority over them."* Jesus motioned us to the side of the road where he sat down, as if to emphasize his next words.

We took our places along beside him. Looking first at each of us, individually and in silence, he continued, softly. *"Not so with you. Instead, whoever wants to become great among you must be your servant, and whoever wants to be first must be slave of all"* (Mark 10:41-44). With that Jesus told us to take our rest. He left, alone, to go to the market place and buy food for the twelve.

Reflections on "Unresolved Conflict"

Jesus approach to conflict among the disciples was neither passive or belligerent. He seemed to understand conflict as a part of the formation process, a teaching and learning moment. In many gospel passages he grasps the moment to illustrate a higher principal and so invites his followers to move through conflict to another place.

In the church of Christ (including the Biblical/historical witness) we tend to respond to conflict as a plague. We either ignore it, hoping our passive response will allow us to pretend it never happened or confront with anger and judgment one or both parties in an attempt to overwhelm, shame or guilt trip them into submission. Either response frustrates the 'sanctifying' possibilities that conflict is pregnant with. We lose the creative moment in which a real understanding of human pain may transcend our angry isolation.

Q: In your experience in the Church, is Terry right?

Q: How can we teach our communities of faith to fight fair and listen well and reverence, always?

Pray for yourself (at a point of conflict) ...or your church, perhaps?

Who Am I?

6 A Pause, Before the Storm

...The Place of Jericho & Bethany, just Before

Invocation:

> Out of deep despair we come to You, O Lord. Hear our cry for help. O Lord Jesus, listen with care to our complaints as we voice them. May your heart be open to our cry for mercy.
>
> Father, if you keep a record of our sins, who could stand in your presence? Who would have a shot at knowing you? But in the Christ, whom you sent, there is forgiveness; **THEREFORE**, you are held in awe. We are aware that sudden destruction comes to those who misuse your forgiving heart. So we wait before you, O Father of life. Within the depths of our inmost being we turn to silence before you. Still our hearts. Help us to long for your coming like the robin who waits for the new day's first light. Help us to wait like a lover longing to see her beloved at the start of a new day. Come, Lord.
>
> O Israel and the Church who follows Jeshua. Let us put our hope in the Father of all, for with the Father is unfailing love and in him is complete

RENEWAL OF OUR LIVES. FATHER-SON-SPIRIT, YOU ARE OUR HOPE. YOU, YOURSELF WILL REDEEM ISRAEL AND YOUR CHURCH FROM ALL OUR SINS. AMEN.

ADAPTED FROM PSALM 130

PSALM OF THE WEEK: PSALM 125

QUOTE OF THE WEEK: ALL THE GOOD YOU WILL DO WILL COME NOT FROM YOU BUT FROM THE FACT THAT YOU HAVE ALLOWED YOURSELF, IN THE OBEDIENCE OF FAITH, TO BE USED BY GOD'S LOVE.

FROM THOMAS MERTON, RE-QUOTED IN "TURN MY MOURNING INTO DANCING" BY HENRI NOUWEN, PG #73

DAILY SCRIPTURES:

MONDAY—MATTHEW 6: 10-13 & JOHN 10: 40-42 & JOSHUA 5: 13-15 & 6: 1-5, 18-19

TUESDAY—MATTHEW 6: 24 & LUKE 19: 11-27 & JOSHUA 7: 1, 19-21, 25-26

WEDNESDAY—MATTHEW 5: 5-7 & LUKE 18: 9-14 & EPHESIANS 4:29-32 & 5: 1-2

THURSDAY—MATTHEW 6: 10 & LUKE 18: 31-43

FRIDAY—MATTHEW 5: 46-48 & LUKE 19: 1-10 & JOHN 11: 7-16

Saturday—Matthew 6: 25-34 & John 11: 17-46

SUNDAY—MATTHEW 5: 5 & 7: 6 & LUKE 19: 28-46 & JOHN 11: 45-57 ISAIAH 44: 24-28 & ZECHARIAH 9: 9-10 & JOHN 12: 1-19

Our Craving for Acceptance
from
Turn My Mourning Into Dancing
by Henri Nouwen
Page #72-74

In the most significant relationships of our lives, ...we discover one another as living reminders of God's presence. Friendship and marriage and relationships among those in the church community become ways to reveal to one another the original, all embracing love of God, in which we participate and of which we become human disclosures.

We stumble on this...in three significant ways. First, we have difficulty because of our intense need to be justified, a need rooted in our craving to be liked and accepted by the significant (or not-so-significant) people in our lives. Many things we think we do for others are in fact the expressions of our drive to discover our identity in the praise of others.

...Activism (is) the second way in which we try to manage others or love with conditions. We end up doing things for others for the sake of...ourselves. This kind of activism gathers merit badges. It is motivated by guilt, by the feeling of being indebted, by the sense of having to earn righteousness or favor—from God or others.

...(The)third stumbling block to truly loving others: our competitiveness... On very subtle

LEVELS WE COMPETE WITHOUT WANTING TO, OFTEN WITHOUT REALIZING IT. WE COMPARE OURSELVES TO OTHERS AND WORRY ABOUT WHAT OTHERS THINK OF US EVEN WHEN WE ARE SERVING OTHERS… WE IMPORT A DRIVE TO ACHIEVE (SUCCEED) INTO OUR WORKS OF MERCY.

Week-6: MONDAY—MATTHEW 6: 10-13 & JOHN 10: 40-42 & JOSHUA 5: 13-15 & 6: 1-5, 18-19

Story 21—Unmasked

We spent the better part of the day in Jericho, old Jericho, just resting. We ate a noon meal at the local market and relaxed in the bright sun. I love dates, especially dates from Jericho, grown in the shaded orchards surrounded by pools of water flowing down from the mountain springs. The arguments and rivalry of our journey since the transfiguration seemed to melt in the embrace of Jericho's hospitality to all the pilgrims making their way to Jerusalem.

That evening we once again made our way out the city following the main water way leading from old Jericho to the Jordan. At one point, near the Jordan, I stopped and turned to take in the view of this beautiful plain. I knew it well from my days with the Baptist. My heart swelled within me and so I sat down under a sycamore tree to think. I thought I knew where our camp site would be. Judas Iscariot stopped as well and took a seat near me, on a rock. We sat in silence, each in his own world.

I knew I was looking at an ancient city that had been here long before my Hebrew cousins came across the Jordan, on dry land, to capture this beautiful valley for Yahweh. I looked at those portions of the city walls still standing and wondered what it must have been like for those first followers of Joshua, walking around the city seven times, blowing trumpets and listening to the laughter and jeering of the people of Jericho as they considered the spectacle in front of them. Did they have an unquestioning belief in Joshua or did they too wonder what he was doing as I had Jeshua, even a couple of weeks before. 'Who am I kidding?' the question forced itself. I was questioning him now, in my heart. 'Why were we staying in this beautiful place when Jeshua's very best friend, Lazarus, was in need? Well, at least his sisters were. And what was Jesus doing? Apparently nothing.' My conscience quickly objected. 'Had not the master told us that Lazarus *"sickness will not end in death'?* "No," he had said, *"it is for God's glory so that God's Son may be glorified through it"* (John 11: 4). I failed to see how our absence could contribute to God's glory, let alone Martha or Mary's wellbeing. But as I looked at Jericho's walls I realized how little faith I still had in my Master's instincts.

"Amazing, isn't it?" My hearts doubts were pulled back into reality by Judas. I'd almost forgot he was near. "Yes it is," I replied. Judas went on, as if speaking to himself. "We just spent the whole day in old Jericho, and there, not two miles' distance is where the real seat of power is!" I quickly turned my heard to see what Judas was talking about. He was looking to our left, not at old Jericho, but at the modern Jericho nestled high on the tell above the old city. It was Herod, the Tetrarch's new winter palace and the administrative capital of the region over which he had charge. Judas went on. "We just wasted a day in old Jericho when it is Herod's city that we need to be making contact with. Jesus brings to the table the very power, spiritual and earthly, that will finally bring down the walls surrounding Israel's heart." He paused and looked in my direction, as if to see my response. Turning back to the old city, I kept my face forward, trying hard not to betray what I was feeling. I had forgotten that Judas Iscariot was a zealot before entering Jeshua's service. The zealots were a relatively recent political and military movement. Their founder, Ezekias (Hezekiah) from a village just east of Galilee had been killed by Herod the Great for insurrection against Rome. Now, his son, Judah of Gamla, just north and east of the Great sea was leading a rebellion against Herod's sons and Rome, trying to usher in the day of Messiah. I knew that Judas believed Jeshua was the Messiah and would be the one to finally and peacefully bring Roman rule to and end and confront Herod's sons with a choice; Follow or be overrun. So, I just kept staring at old Jericho, not allowing myself to glance toward either Judas or Herodian Jericho, Herod Antipas' capital. After some silence and feigning a casual spirit which betrayed my real feelings I rose and spoke directly to Judas. "Brother, let us go! Talk like that will get us killed! Besides," I lowered my voice, perhaps revealing my own fears, "Jeshua knows what he is doing."

My heart sank as I made my way back to camp with the other ten and Jeshua. My own heart was not so far removed from Judas's heart in the matter of trust. His mind was filled with treason while my troubled thoughts had the markings of betrayal. I knew we had both been unmasked by the memory of old walls falling.

Reflections on "Unmasked"

Q: What has been your greatest disappointment with God, since starting to follow Jeshua?

Q: Is it an issue of trust? ...How so? ...Why not?

> *"(Our) Activism comes from an unbelief that insists that God does not or cannot move and act; it wants to replace God's supposed slowness or inaction with our activity. But we should intend that what we do to help and serve and minister does not create in the absence of God, but respond to what God is already bringing into being.*
> Henri Nouwen, "Our Craving for Acceptance" from "Turn My Mourning Into Dancing," Pages 72-74.

Q: Do you have a firm belief that God is active in the city? ...At your place of employment? ...Inside the injustices of modernity?   Reflect and pray:

Week-6: TUESDAY—MATTHEW 6: 24 & LUKE 19: 11-27 & JOSHUA 7: 1, 19-21, 25-26

STORY 22—THE KINGDOM

It was now the second day since Martha and Mary had sent their servant warning us of Lazarus approaching death. 'Surely,' I thought, 'Jeshua would respond today.' But he didn't give any hint of concern for Lazarus as we made our way into old Jericho. We were just outside the ancient walls that Joshua had brought down. We were in an open field, not far from the waters feeding the gardens of this city when Jesus stopped. A small crowd of about a hundred or so had gathered outside the walls waiting for Jesus, knowing that he was still in the area and would likely pass this way as he continued his journey to the festival in Jerusalem.

Looking first at Judas and then me, he moved into the center of the crowd and began a story, lifting his voice. "From the time of Joshua's triumph over this ancient city Yahweh has sought to bring down walls that lie between his children and between us and Him." I looked around and noticed the intense interest of the crowd. This was Jericho, a city rich in dreams of Messiah and of the age to come, of the next Joshua. Jeshua seemed to be looking south and west toward Herodian Jericho, the new administrative capital Herod Antipas was building. Most of Jericho's business community had moved to this new part of the ancient city, nestled further into the hill country. Suddenly, Jeshua began a story. It was one we had heard and often, but with a new twist that his listeners were sure to catch.

"A man of noble birth went to a distant country to have himself appointed king," he began while still looking toward Herod's capital. "While gone he entrusted to ten of his servants ten minas." My mind quickly calculated; 'sufficient money for the needs of any of his subjects, about three months' wages. But to the nobleman, it was a small risk'. *"Put this money to work," he said, "until I come back."* Now Jesus turned toward old Jericho and the towns people gathering still closer to him so as not to miss a word. Jesus continued. *"But his subjects hated him and sent a delegation after him to say, 'We don't want this man to be our king.'"*

Looking to my left I noticed that Judas Iscariot's interest had just peaked, as had mine. Judas took a step closer to Jesus, his eyes looking hopeful. Mine were filled with fear, I'm sure. Every citizen of Jericho knew who my master was speaking of, for Herod the Great's son and Herod Antipas's brother, Archaleaus, made such a pilgrimage to Rome upon his father's death. He went to visit with Caesar and have himself appointed king in his father's place. And right behind him went a delegation headed by Antipas and members from the Sanhedrin, the Jewish ruling council, eager to block Herod Archelaus's rise to the position of his father. For they knew him to be as cruel as his father. He had been responsible for the killing of 3,000 Pharisees soon after his father's death. Suddenly, I thought, 'maybe Judas is right. Perhaps Jesus will now complete his mission as Joshua of old.'

Jesus sat down under a tree, the crowd gathering in. I was glad that the story would finish in the relative quiet of a small crowd gathering close, until I looked up and noticed one of the Pharisees standing near the back, arms folded and with look of grave concern. Next to him stood a man of some import. His clothing was made of fine cloth and the color was a deep purple. 'Possibly from Herod Antipas own court.' I wondered as the reality of it all hit me. 'Jeshua is walking very near sedition.' I assumed they felt the same.

"Now," Jeshua looked up into the longing faces and continued. "Now, the nobleman was made king, in spite of the objection of his subjects and returned home. Then he sent for the servants to find out what they had gained with their ten minas. *The first came and said, 'Sir, your mina has eared ten more...' 'Well done, my good servant!' his master replied. 'Because you have been trustworthy in a very small matter, take charge of ten cities.' The second came and said, 'Sir, your mina has earned five more.' His master answered, 'You take charge of five cities.' Then another servant came and said 'Sir, here is your mina; I have kept it laid away in a piece of cloth. I was afraid of you, because you are a hard man. You take out what you did not put in and reap what you did not sow.'"* Jesus shifted, moving his arm as it rested on top of his knee, for emphasis. "To this servant his master replied, *'I will judge you by your own words, you wicked servant! You knew, did you, that I am a hard man, taking out what I did not put in, and reaping what I did not sow? Why then didn't you put my money on deposit, so that when I came back, I could have collected it, with interest?'* Now Jesus stood and made his way into the crowd as he spoke. "Then the nobleman *said to those standing by, 'Take his mina away from him and give it to the one who has ten!'"* Jesus turned slowly, his arms open before him, giving instruction. "I tell you plainly. The kingdom of God is coming and soon! In fact, it is at the door." I glanced at Judas who was smiling broadly. Turning directly toward Judas Iscariot and speaking more softly, almost pleading, he continued. "But it does not come as men think. It does not come through those whose robes are purple. But to those who hear the words of my Father and obey." Jesus once again moved toward Judas and placing his right hand on Judas left shoulder as a support he spoke past him. "Open your heart to God's voice." Jeshua's voice softened as his face turned toward Judas ear. "Like Achan of old, before Joshua, confess the silver you have kept to yourself. Repent of the purple clothes you have coveted. And unlike Joshua, my Father will have mercy. For the kingdom of my Father comes in love, poured out." Looking back, I now realize that Jeshua was pleading for Judas heart, for he was a thief. Jesus continued, now moving directly and purposefully to the

Pharisee, still standing near the back. He stood frozen as Jesus approached. Speaking more loudly so that all could hear, Jesus said. "I tell you that to everyone who has this love, more will be given, but as for the one who has nothing but love of himself, even what he has will be taken from him." And turning directly toward the one dressed in fine cloth of deep purple Jesus finished. "And the king? What did he do? He called in all those who had traveled some distance to oppose him. *Bring them here, he commanded and kill them in front of me.*"

(Note: Selection above *in Italics* from Luke 19: 11-27)

Reflections on "The Kingdom"

Consider this scene and place yourself in it?

Q: What is the import of Jesus ability to tells stories in a cultural, political and social context that made the kingdom live? ...Have we lost that art? ...Do you have it? ...Do you live a 'relevant and challenging gospel'?

Q: Who in this crowd would you have been?
- ❖ Judas Iscariot
- ❖ The Pharisee
- ❖ John
- ❖ The crowd listening

...How so?

Pray and ask that God will anoint the Church (you included) with the ability to reflect Jesus thoughtfully and in a way that communicates to our post-modern culture.

Week-6: WEDNESDAY—Matthew 5: 5-7 & Luke 18: 9-14 & Ephesians 4:29-32 & 5: 1-2

My Thoughts 14—Compassion's Source

"We discover… that for all our good intentions, compassion does not form the true basis of our lives. Compassion does not come as our spontaneous response but goes against the grain. We might wonder if it is humanly possible!

Such a view has a healthy consequence. Compassion in its fullest sense can be attributed only to God… It is because Jesus was not dependent on people, but only on God, that he could be so close to people, so concerned, so confronting, so healing, so caring. He related to people for their own sake, not his own…"

From "Is Compassion Possible?" by Henri Nouwen in "Turn My Mourning Into Dancing," Page #74-75

We as a culture have lost the art of 'reverence'… the ability to treat our enemies or those with whom we disagree with the civility and respect deserved as a daughter and son of Adam and Eve.

Just look at the Republican 2016 debates with Donald Trump at center and we have a living picture of a world beyond reverence. Listen to our President who impugns not simply the ideas of his opponents but their motive as well, as do many of the talk radios stars (left and right) who occupy our public space. Sadly, much of the evangelical church has joined in the disrespect, certain of the 'rightness' of its message and equally certain of the 'wrongness' of its sceptics.

What is missing? Compassion steeped in 'reverence.' The reverence of a Mother Theresa who sees in the face of all she sees, Jesus.

Compassion begins and ends with an understanding of each—every—all humans as created in the image of God and deserving of tender respect on that basis alone. It is the heart of Jesus who invites (not commands) us to come to him, for he is *"gentle and humble in heart"* (Matthew 11: 29). It is a humility of God that in the end allows us to land ourselves in a self-created hell, void of God because we revere something/someone which displaces God's place in all our relations. Why? Because our choices matter and are valued even when they exclude God's actual presence.

So compassion doesn't ask the homeless 'why' they are in such a place unless and until we have lived inside their space and are invited to be helpful… and we cannot be helpful so long as we see ourselves in a place above because we live in rented or owned homes and are somehow, thereby, worthy. A compassionate person sees themselves as broken, wounded and living lost; except for the ever and always presence of the Love of God who enters our darkest night 'as one' with us shedding light and granting us/everyone with ever new possibilities for wholeness.

It is that 'reverence' for 'human pain' (in which we all participate) that allows us to receive as well as give when we are in mission mode; helping others who in some way who are more vulnerable than we. As we listen and receive the graces and gifts of those with whom we minister we are overcome by our common humanity and the gifts of God that grace everyone. It is called compassion which is really 'reverence' living inside the human story.

Reflections on "Compassion's Source"

"Real ministry starts taking place when we bring others in touch with more than we ourselves are—the center of being, the reality of the unseen—the Father who is the source of life and healing."

From "Is Compassion Possible?" by Henri Nouwen in "Turn My Mourning into Dancing," Page #74-75

Nouwen is really suggesting that it is the narrative of God with us, in us—accepting and healing our broken spaces that is the real source of our ability to gift anyone anything. It is this narrative of God that people are hungry to connect with, not us.

Q: Do people see God in the narrative of your life? …How so? …Why not?

Terry makes the case the 'compassion' is not possible without 'reverence'… where judgment has been abandoned in the awareness of our mutual human needs.

Q: What about this definition of compassion? …Is it right?

Q: If so, have you even begun to minister?

Your thoughts…turn it to prayer.

Week-6: THURSDAY—MATTHEW 6: 10 & LUKE 18: 31-43

STORY 23—COMPASSION

Jesus had been gone most of the day. Following the morning teachings and his call to repent of everything but love, he had turned and walked away toward the waterway intersecting old Jericho and the Jordan. He sat down, alone, to pray. We immediately surrounded, at some distance, protecting him from those who might press in. Toward noon he went for a walk and instructed us to again enter Jericho and eat. Judas Iscariot, who had the money purse led the way.

It was early in the afternoon when Jeshua showed up and motioned us to follow. He was headed out of the old city and turning south toward Herod's new Jericho. Judas Iscariot was eager to catch up. He had been anticipating the moment when we might enter Herod's capital city, his winter palace. I stayed back, some distance behind. Another, even larger crowd had gathered around Jesus and were walking with him. Some were pilgrims making their way through the Herodian Jericho and up into the hill country on the road to Jerusalem. But most were citizens of old and new Jericho, waiting for some teaching or miracle perhaps.

I was in deep thought. 'The kingdom of God is coming and soon!' These were the words I recalled from this morning's teachings. They were echoing in the chambers of my heart, together with other words of my master. *'They will flog him, insult him, spit on him and kill him'* (Luke 18: 32). My heart sank. 'How could both of these be true? How could the kingdom of our Father come through these terrible events?'

My mind searched for what my heart could not admit. 'What had Jesus said this morning about the kingdom?' I remembered still more. 'It does not come as men think.' Then, suddenly, I could hear his words, as if for the first time. 'From the time of Joshua's triumph over this ancient city Yahweh has sought to bring down walls that lie between us…' My heart raced to catch up with my thoughts. 'All of the last three years in Jeshua's footsteps were about this one thing. Restoring what was broken, bringing to nothing the walls that divide us.'

Without realizing it, I had passed beyond old Jericho's walls and was about half way toward the new city. The crowd was now well in front of me. What had awakened me to my surroundings was the sound of a man arguing, perhaps crying out. He was repeating over and again, *"Jesus, Son of David, have mercy on me!"* (Luke 18:38). The crowd around him was trying to quiet him. "Shut up!" They shouted back. They obviously knew him, but did not see him. That was plain for they cried out. "For we want to see him too and hear what he has to say!" I was now within ten feet of the man and could see he was a beggar, crippled and blind. He was standing, awkwardly, unable to stand fully or upright. *"Jesus!"* he cried out even louder, ignoring those who did not see him, anyway. *"Jesus! Son of David! Have mercy on me!"* (Luke 18:38). A man from the crowd stepped forward and shoved him and then turning, walked away. There was even some scoffing laughter. Filled with anger I turned to help him. Taking his arm and steadying him, I asked. "What's your name?" He looked in my direction, his eyes unable to focus. But his face was filled with the look of shock. "My name?" he asked. "You want to know my name?" "Yes, of course." My heart felt a compassion I had never known before. Often, I have wanted to do good things, in order to be good. Never had I recalled being good. Immediately Jeshua's words re-echoed in my mind. 'Yahweh has sought to bring down walls that lie between us… they will flog him and insult him, spit on him, and…'

From some distance I heard Jeshua's voice. "Bring him to me." I was aware that the crowd had stopped and some were now turned towards me, or maybe, not me. Again, Jesus spoke. "The man who called out my name and cried for mercy. Bring him!" The crippled man also heard and was attempting to search for his cane, now lost. Instead, I took him by the arm and simply said, "Come, I'll help you find him." As the crowd was making way, some reluctantly, we hobbled our way toward Jeshua. "Bartimaeus." I turned toward him, pausing for just a moment. "Bartimaeus," he continued. "My name." Smiling within and without, though he could see neither, I responded. "It is good to meet you, Bartimaeus." I knew I meant it. I also knew something of the Kingdom of my Papa and of Jeshua's papa had entered into me in that moment. And I remembered another thing from my Master. *"Your kingdom come,"* he had prayed often. *"Your will be done on earth as it is in heaven"* (Matthew 6:10).

Reflections on "Compassion"

The heart of compassion lies, not in the act of kindness, but in the feeling of seeing in another's need your own. There is a relationship between compassion and mercy. Between mercy given and mercy received. It is those who understand themselves as sinners who can minister alongside other sinners, without judgment.

Compassion means being in the same boat with another, not because you are humbling yourself from a position higher and stepping down, but because you are already in the boat. You live or drown together. The only difference is that you know enough to look for help. In fact, you know enough to know that the one you are trying to help may have already found the help you need.

Q: Have you ever ministered with this sense of 'being in the same boat'? ...How so? ...Why not?

Q: Who is the most compassionate person you know? ...What makes them so compelling?

Pray that God will pour out upon your and your church this **'in the same boat'** kind of compassion.

Week-6: FRIDAY—MATTHEW 5: 46-48 & LUKE 19: 1-10 & JOHN 11: 7-16

STORY 24—LIVING WITH PURPOSE

As Jesus turned and continued his journey towards Herodian Jericho, I stayed with Bartimaeus, helping to gather his cane and belongings. As before, I began to assist his steps. However, it was soon apparent to both of us that his walk had changed. With each step his legs seem to gather strength and his stride became increasingly, well, normal. Bartimaeus looked at me and stopped. He let go of my arm and set out on his own. He was perfectly well in body as well as sight. Quickly we gathered his belongings. He left his cane to another beggar nearby and we turned to follow Jesus.

Just outside of the new city was a giant sycamore tree. Jesus was gathered under it, but looking up as if speaking to someone. We ran to catch up. Bartimaeus was delighted. The crowd had already turned its attention away from him and to Jesus, so they had not noticed that he was no longer crippled.

Approaching the edge of the crowd I could make out Matthew's voice. "Master," he was saying. "This is my friend, Zacchaeus." I noticed a degree of shock among a few, who evidently knew of the man. "Like me, his profession is the collecting of taxes." "Yea, I am one of those this Roman lover cheated!" A man yelled from somewhere to my left. I had now made my way to the center being careful to keep Bartimaeus just behind. Matthew quickly continued his introduction, so as to not further embarrass his friend.

Interestingly, his friend Zacchaeus, I think he had said, was up and resting on the arm of the tree. "Rabbi, I have known Zacchaeus for many years. Of all the Roman collectors, he was the most honest. Certainly, better than I." You could hear murmurs of disapproval, subtle, but real, at Matthew's defense. Jesus stepped in and, as usual, upped the risk. Speaking directly to Zacchaeus he said. *"Zacchaeus, come down immediately. I must stay at your house today"* (Luke 19: 5b). At that the murmur turned to a shudder with some hisses and obvious side conversations in the crowd. For a moment I felt a little frightened. Looking down at Bartimaeus I could see only curiosity. He was evidently comfortable with open hostility.

Quickly Zacchaeus made his way to ground level. He did not stand over four feet. I now knew why he had climbed into the tree to begin with. Turning to Jesus and with a voice of authority he called out. *"Lord,"* he hesitated, not sure of what address to give. So he repeated himself with more emphasis upon the word, as you would in the presence of a majesty. "My Lord! *Here and now I give half of my possessions to the poor, and...,"* looking around for the one who had charged him with cheating he continued. "And, *if I have cheated anybody out of anything*, please come and see me. *I will pay back four times the amount"* (Luke 19: 8). All eyes turned to Jeshua, whose eyes sparkled with compassion and an air of authority that I often noticed when he is teaching. *"Today,"* Jesus began, *"salvation has come to this house, because this man, too, is a son of Abraham."* Then lifting his voice to all present he emphasized. *"For the Son of Man came to seek and to save what was lost* (Luke 19: 9), to repair what is broken and bring to nothing the gigantic walls between his children and between all of us and my Father in heaven!" Turning back to Zacchaeus he said. "In my Father's house the sound of a great trumpet is blowing in honor of this moment." Jeshua hesitated for a moment and looked around the crowd gathered before continuing. His eyes were now a little sad, as if wondering if any caught the real miracle today, of walls falling at the sound of a heavenly trumpet. I did get it, maybe for the first time. "Now, Zacchaeus, son of Abraham, take me to your home."

Later that evening, after the party with the twelve, Zacchaeus and his friends and Bartimaeus, Jeshua gathered the twelve to himself. We were pretty tired after a long day and ready for the deep sleep we would enjoy in this spacious home. "Tomorrow," he began, "we will make our way back to Judea." *"But Rabbi,"* Judas Iscariot spoke up. "What of Herod Antipas? I have discovered that he is in his home and I am certain would give audience. *A short while ago the Jews tried to stone you and yet you are going back there...?"* Almost pleading, he added, "Without the protection of Antipas? I am sure if he only knew better your mission..." Jesus lifted his hand, directing Judas to stop. Judas looked visibly offended. "Judas," he began. *"Are there not twelve hours of daylight."* I thought to myself, 'well, yes, when working for you.' Jesus continued. *"A man who walks by day will not stumble, for he sees by this world's light. It is when he walks by night that he stumbles, for he has no light"* (John 11: 8-10).

I could see that Jeshua's allegory did not satisfy Judas Iscariot's concern. But Jeshua added. "Our friend Lazarus has fallen asleep; but I am going there to wake him up," Philip responded. "Lord, if he sleeps, he will get better." Jesus replied plainly. "Lazarus is dead, and for your sake I am glad I was not there, so that you may believe. But, now we must go to him." I think most of us thought we were returning to grieve with Martha and Mary and Lazarus friends. 'Why,' I wondered again. 'Why had Jeshua delayed?' I glanced over and saw Bartimaeus in deep conversation with Zacchaeus and smiled. 'That at least is part of the reason', I thought.

Reflections on "Living with Purpose"

Reflections on 'Living with Purpose:

Q: Have you ever thought of the relationship between Zacchaeus salvation and his probable knowing of Matthew, a tax collector?

Q: In both stories, Terry is writing in human details which involve the disciple's thoughts, feelings and inter-action with the persons Jesus is relating to. How does this strike you? ...Why?

Q: Have you ever felt like a central player inside the unfolding story of Jesus in our times? ...How so? ...Why not?

Pray and ask that God will weave you into the unfolding narrative of salvation in the earth? Perhaps you already have a sense of it. Offer thanks, if you do.

Week-6: SATURDAY— MATTHEW 6: 25-34 & JOHN 11: 17-46

STORY 25—NEW LIFE

For the first time since Mary's arrival and the mourning party with her, the occasional howls of crying and the softer and more deeply felt gentle tears stopped. It was the silence that comes in the early morning, just before the awakening of the sun and birds to a new day. It is an extreme stillness that penetrates the heart. And so it was, now.

Martha and Mary were relatively well off and could afford the professional mourners who knew how to blend their dramatic efforts with the family's and friend's grief so as to not overwhelm but support and deepen the sense of sorrow. Jesus, standing about half way between the family with those mourning and the now open grave had just lifted his arms to heaven in prayer. I heard his words, for I stood not six feet away, standing sideways to him, able to take in the whole scene.

His prayer had been simple. *"Father, I thank you that you have heard me. I knew that you always hear me, but I said this for the benefit of the people standing here, that they may believe that you sent me"* (John 11: 41b-42). My thoughts once again turned to Elijah on Carmel and simple prayer that had brought fire down from the heavens and the rain that followed. I also wondered, 'how can the others standing near benefit, when only I hear?' I had not yet come to realize the power of memory to recreate as the Church told and retold her stories. Then Jeshua, leaving one hand facing heaven and the other Lazarus simply commanded, *"Lazarus, come out!"* (John 11: 43b)

I turned my head toward the grave. The noise of a rushing wind seemed to echo against the inner chambers of the grave, built into the hill side, above ground. There was apparent movement within. The stench of the decaying body, now exposed by the removal of the heavy stone blocking the family grave was now forgotten. All of us were spell bound, frightened, hopeful. Energy ran through my body. Suddenly, Lazarus appeared, his face partially exposed, but bound by the grave cloths tightly wound around his body. Jesus simply turned to the mourners and said, *"Take off the grave clothes and let him go"* (John 11: 44b).

What happened next was sheer pandemonium. Glancing around, I noticed some on their knees, hands raised to the heavens. Gasps and murmuring enveloped all around. Most of the twelve stood motionless, astonished that the impossible had become possible. Judas Iscariot's response troubled me. His arms were folded. A wry smile appeared on his face. You could read his thoughts. 'Now, no one will stand in our way!' I turned to Jeshua, who was being pressed upon by the now hundred or more gathered. The news was already bringing others from the village. In all the adulation I noticed that Jesus simply wept, gently. From compassion for the family or over the irony he knew he had released, I could not tell. 'This will be his last miracle,' I thought. 'Either the elders will receive him or be determined, now, to…' I cut off the implications.

Then, almost as one, the twelve began to do what we were good at. We began to gently create order from the chaos, placing ourselves, almost unnoticed, between the Master and his adoring crowd. Very soon, Martha and Mary brought Lazarus to Jeshua and so we made room. Lazarus stunk. But no one seemed to care about the fading odor. Jeshua was the first to speak, addressing Martha, reminding her of her own words minutes before and now with a gentle smile. *"Your brother will rise again."* Jesus wiped a tear away as he spoke. Martha laughed in response. *"Yes, at the last day."* Jeshua stopped and looking directly at her announced. "Behold, Martha, it is here! *I am the resurrection and the life."*

And now turning to all present he repeated what he had first spoken to Martha, only in private. *"And whoever lives and believes in me will never die!"*(John 11:23-27) Judas Iscariot broke in on the conversation, abruptly. "Yes, Master. Now all Jerusalem will follow." Jeshua, looking straight into Judas's eyes and heart countered. "Will they, Judas? Will they?" With that, he turned to leave.

Reflections on "New Life"

Q: Where do you see yourself in this story?
- The professional mourners
- The family-friends of Mary and Martha
- Mary
- Judas Iscariot
- Martha
- John the beloved

…How so?

Q: What grave clothes need to be removed in your life?

Consider what it is God is working on in your life…How God wants to form the Jesus narrative in you and pray:

Week-6: SUNDAY—MATTHEW 5: 5 & 7: 6 & LUKE 19: 28-46
& JOHN 11: 45-57 ISAIAH 44: 24-28 & ZECHARIAH 9: 9-10
& JOHN 12: 1-19

STORY 26—CONFRONTATION

Judas Iscariot's face looked ashen. My own, I'm certain, appeared no different. If Lazarus resurrection had offered any hope of a way out the approaching sorrow, it surely vanished in the anger Jesus had now demonstrated within his Papa's house. That seemed apparent.

Now it was over. The money changers booths were scattered all over the Court of the Gentiles. Sheep and doves were fleeing their masters as Jeshua pushed their cages aside, in what appeared a fit of rage. A near riot had ensued as some of the disciples joined and a handful of Jerusalem's inhabitants picked up the feeling, some adding their curses and others only feelings of disgust.

'Jesus clearly had good reason,' I thought to myself. The very poorest could barely afford the outrageous prices the house of Caiaphas demanded for the sheep and doves, sold for sacrifice. All knew that the high standards of the temple priests stationed at the Master Gate, when inspecting the animals brought by the pilgrims to this Holy Place, were driven in part by the fact that the High Priest controlled a patronage system of vendors who operated just outside the Temple. These vendors had a near monopoly on the exchange rates of Roman and Greek coins to Temple coins and the purchase of pre-approved animals for sacrifice. Did I say outside? Well, they were supposed to be outside the Court of the Gentiles, on the approach to the Temple Mount.

Only under Caiaphas and only in the last few years had they been allowed to encroach into the Court of the Gentiles.

It had all started very differently. Judas Iscariot, together with Simon who had been a zealot before following Jeshua, had led the way. The news of Lazarus resurrection had spread throughout the region of Bethpage, Bethany and Jerusalem. At every hour thousands were pouring into the Holy City that went from 50,000 to 200,000 or more during the festivals surrounding Passover. All of us took our ques from the crowd and Jeshua, who had secured, on a previous trip, a foul of a donkey, evidently for this purpose. The Palm branches we had purchased in Jericho, together with those of other pilgrims were now filling the air and being spread on the path before Jeshua. Even the tunics of the rich and poor were being laid before him. Zechariah's vision was clearly at hand. 'Had not Jeshua predicted the same two days ago, to Martha?', I thought. '"Behold, Martha, it is here!" he had said, meaning 'The last day, the day of God's kingdom.'

All was smiles! All, but the Pharisees, a small party sent by the Elders to watch and report. As we near the bottom of the Mount of Olives and were making our way across the Kidron Valley our numbers increased. I would guess more than a thousand were surrounding. One of the Pharisees, 'almost in panic,' I thought, spoke up. "Teacher!", he yelled above the noise. *"Teacher, rebuke your disciples!"* I was walking right beside Jesus, on his left. It just dawned on me, James was on his right. Anyway, Jeshua replied. *"I tell you, if they keep quiet, the stones will cry out"*(Luke 19: 39b-40).

The Pharisee did not look pleased. His worst fears were coming down around him. We were now making our way up the Temple Mount. The Temple guards were clearly watching. I had been watching the activity along the upper wall. More were gathering. In the distance at the top of the Mount were Roman soldiers on horse, perhaps fifty. Their presence was clearly to remind all of their vigilant presence. But, so far, they were leaving the crowd alone. 'And probably would, so long as we were peaceful,' I surmised. Only later, from Nicodemius and Joseph of Arimathea would I discover that the High Priest, just the day before, had suggested that *"it is better... that one man die for the people than that the whole nation perish."* Many years later, upon reflection, I realized that he was speaking a prophesy, as high priest, *that Jesus would die for the Jewish nation and not only for that nation but also for the scattered children of God,* all of them, *to bring them together and make them one"* (John 11: 50, 52).

Having taken in the entire scene and sensing the same danger that the Pharisees felt, I stopped my joyous celebration and sobered. It was only then that I noticed Jeshua's own change of spirit. With tears pouring gently down his cheeks and speaking in a loud voice he cried, *"If you, even you, had known on this day what would bring you peace—but now it is hidden from your eyes"* (Luke 19: 42). I turned my full attention to him. We were now at the top of the Temple mount. We would either proceed into Jerusalem and move toward the centers of Rome's power or proceed into the Temple. Judas, leading on, had made up his mind and was clearly leading the crowd in the direction of the city, almost arrogantly past the Roman soldiers, as if to taunt them into a reaction. Jeshua had stopped and looking around, continued his plea for Jerusalem's attention. Then he dismounted and on foot made his way toward the Eastern Gate. At one point, just before entering he turned and spoke. I glanced and noticed Judas, now at the back of the crowd, in rapt attention, wondering what his Master was doing? *"It is written,"* Jesus said, *"My house will be a house of prayer for all nations, but you have made it a den of robbers"* (Luke 19: 46). With that, he turned and entered the court of the Gentiles in righteous anger. 'It has begun," was all that came to mind.

Reflections on "Confrontation"

Q: Where do you see yourself in this story?
- ❖ John the beloved
- ❖ Pharisees
- ❖ Roman soldiers
- ❖ Judas Iscariot
- ❖ Jesus
- ❖ The vendors in the Temple

…How so?

Q: Does our worship, today, reflect more the spirit of Judas Iscariot or of Jeshua? …How so? …How about our missions—Judas or Jeshua?

Reflect on your answers and ask that God might cleanse your own inner sanctuary:

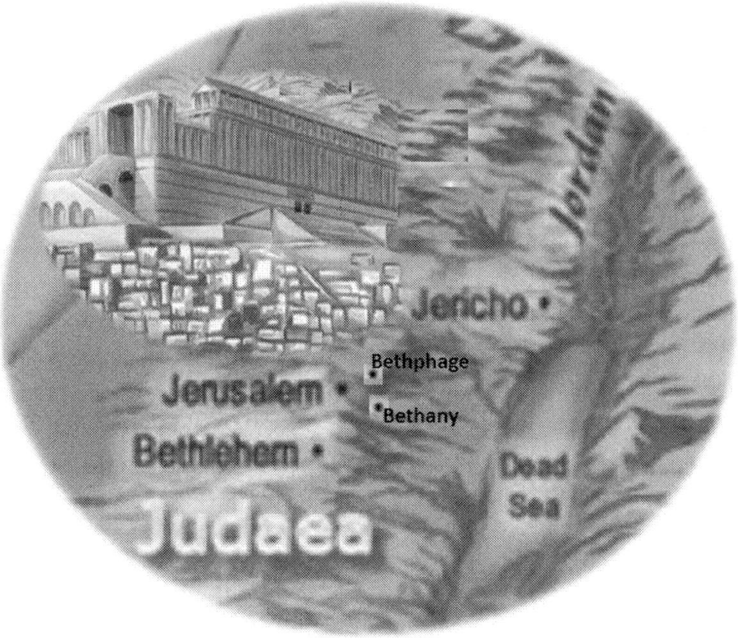
Jordan
Jericho
Bethphage
Jerusalem
Bethany
Bethlehem
Dead Sea
Judaea

7 THE CUP

...Will you also Drink with Me?

INVOCATION:

PRAISE THE LORD! ALL OF US, LORD, WHO SERVE, EVEN IN THE SMALLEST WAY. WE WHO LOVE YOUR HOUSE, HER ALTARS AND WINDOWS, HER OFFERINGS AND FELLOWSHIP, HER COMFORTS AND SORROWS. WE REMAIN, LORD, INSIDE YOUR HOUSE, YOUR STORY, YOUR CITY AND PRAISE YOU.

WE LIFT OUR HANDS LORD, IN YOUR SANCTUARY. DAY AND NIGHT, LET US PRAISE YOU WITH HANDS OF SERVICE TO THE LONELY AND POOR, TO THE WOUNDED AND BROKEN. LET OUR HANDS WORK IN YOUR HOUSE, THE CITY OF YOUR LOVE, SO THAT WHEN WE GATHER FOR WORSHIP, PRAISE FLOWS FROM THE SERVICE OF OUR HANDS.

MAY YOU LORD, CREATOR OF ALL THAT IS, IN THE HEAVENS AND ON EARTH, BLESS US. BLESS US LORD FROM ZION, FROM INSIDE YOUR STORY LIVED IN THE CITY. AMEN.

ADAPTED FROM PSALM 134

PSALM OF THE WEEK: PSALM 122

QUOTE OF THE WEEK: QUOTE OF THE WEEK: WHEN OUR LOVE GROWS FROM GOD'S LOVE WE NO LONGER DIVIDE PEOPLE INTO THOSE WHO DESERVE IT AND THOSE WHO DON'T.

FROM THOMAS MERTON, RE-QUOTED IN "TURN MY MOURNING INTO DANCING" BY HENRI NOUWEN, PG #88

DAILY SCRIPTURES:

MONDAY—MATTHEW 7: 7-12 & ZECHARIAH 12: 1-9 & ISAIAH 1: 21-31 & LUKE 13: 34–35 & LUKE 20: 1-8

TUESDAY—MATTHEW 7: 28-29 & ISAIAH 5: 1-7 & LUKE 19: 47-48 & 20: 9-19

WEDNESDAY—MATTHEW 6: 10 & ISAIAH 4: 2-6 & MARK 4: 30-32 & 11: 12-14, 20-25 & JOHN 15: 1-2

THURSDAY—MATTHEW 5: 43-45 & MARK 14: 1-11 & JOHN 13: 1-16

FRIDAY—MATTHEW 6: 9-13 & LUKE 22: 7-23 & JOHN 13: 16-38 & 14: 1-6

Saturday—Matthew 5: 5 & 7: 7 & Zechariah 13: 7 & John 14: 30, 31 & 15: 1-4 & Mark 14: 32-42 & John 17: 1-7,16-23

SUNDAY—MATTHEW 5: 17-18 & PSALM 22: 1-19 & ZECHARIAH 12: 10 & 13: 1 & JOHN 18: 12-14, 19-24, 28 & 19: 16-42 & MATTHEW 26: 57-64

Twin Agents of Good
When Solitude Meets Solitude
From
Turn My Mourning Into Dancing
By Henri Nouwen
Page #76-83

…How do we move to a place of deep and transforming love? How can experiencing more fully the joys and pains of other people lead us from our dungeon of self and bring us greater joy? How can it bring healing to our fractured relationships? How can God's compassion become ours? We can love only because we have first been loved. In prayer Jesus finds a lonely place where this first love is realized. We can serve people only when we do not make our total sense of self dependent on their response.

This approach can take root in us with two disciplines. Solitude… Solitude means that our aloneness sometimes does not come as a sad fact needing healing but rather offers a place where God comes to bring communion… It means daring to stand in God's presence. Not to guard time simply to be alone, but alone in God's company….

To solitude we add the twin discipline of silence. We participate in the life of the Spirit through all we hear and say—and what we determine not to hear and say. For our listening in silence can manifest the Spirit within and among us, just as surely as our words of salvation and our acts of healing…

Week-7: MONDAY—MATTHEW 7: 7-12 & ZECHARIAH 12: 1-9 & ISAIAH 1: 21-31 & LUKE 13: 34–35 & LUKE 20: 1-8

STORY 27—THE TREMBLING CUP

Early the next morning Jeshua rose. It was about the fourth watch of the night. I woke up, from a rather fitful sleep, the events of the previous day swirling around in my heart and racing into my mind. So I got up and from a distance followed my master. It was not long before he noticed and turning, simply waved his hand to come. We walked up into the hillside, the moon's light, our only guide. After about an hour, before the day's first light, we found ourselves cresting the Mount of Olives, with a panoramic view of Jerusalem. Jesus rested himself against a giant and old olive tree and simply looked. I found a rock, just in front of him and sat down, taking in the shadows of the city in the silver threads of light crossing her. She was beautiful.

Just before dawn and about the time of the first rooster's crow I heard Jeshua pleading, softly, but distinctly. I could not tell if it was a prayer or simply the deep feeling of the soul of One who speaks from beyond time. *"O... Jerusalem,"* he began. At first the words seem to come in pain, with some difficulty. *"Jerusalem..."* He paused. *"You who kill the prophets..."* Now his words gained in intensity and rhythm, like the cadence of a drummer slowly picking up his beat. *"You, who stone those sent to you,* and refuse those who pleaded with you." Now Jeshua stepped away from the tree and went to the very edge of the hill. The moon was now settled into its bed and the first ray of sun light was striking the red earth casting an orange color across the temple mount. For the half of a watch, he stood, silent, watching, waiting. Then, slowly raising his arms, Jesus began to plead in a loud voice. *"How often I have longed to gather your children together as a hen gathers her chicks under her wings..."* Lowering his arms and his head, he whispered, *"but you were not willing!"* (Luke 13: 34)

Jeshua turned away from the city and looked down upon me. I have never seen such sadness in human eyes. Not before. Not since.

Reflections on "The Trembling Cup"

In the Biblical narrative, places matter. The land as well as her people are sacred and need the prayerful watch of God's people.

Q: Have you ever wept over the city? ...Why not? ...How so?

Q: Why was Jerusalem so important to the Trinity of God?

Consider the city or village or community in which you live; Its promise, Its needs. Pray for your community.

Week-7: TUESDAY—MATTHEW 7: 28-29 & ISAIAH 5: 1-7 & LUKE 19: 47-48 & 20: 9-19

STORY 28—BITTER WINE

The Court of the women was filled to capacity. Jesus sat on the steps leading into the Holy Place. Everyone was intent on his words, knowing that a great prophet or, as many believed, the Messiah sat before them. The story of Lazarus's resurrection at Jesus command was by now known by all, although the stories surrounding differed wildly.

Looking around I noticed, first, how comfortable the children were in Jeshua's presence. For the first time in our three-year mission it hit me. They felt safe in his presence. Mothers and fathers gathered near, watching him bless their children. He would speak with a child and ask questions of their village or home. Often laughter would flow from their response. Then he would gather the child up onto his lap or near his heart and pray to his Papa, invoking blessing. All eyes were fixed, all intent, most hungry. Looking past the throng of people and to the left and right of Jesus I noticed the Pharisees, Sadducees and the officials of the Temple. Almost to a person their arms were closed, their faces betraying their hostility.

Suddenly, Jeshua motioned all the children to him. "Come," he said, "and I will tell you a story." The quiet murmurs of the audience slowly died. All hearts now froze in rapt attention. "A young man," he began, holding one child to his heart. "fell in love. He was rich and owned much land. He wanted to give to his beloved the finest wine for their wedding day, which approached. All the village anticipated the day when the groom would gather his friends in a joyful parade and make their way to the bride's home to gather her up into his arms and present her for marriage, before the priest." Some of the children giggled at the idea. But all knew that in the villages of Judea and Galilee, even Samaria, that is exactly what a groom would do. The groom, with the help of his papa would build their room onto the family home, surrounding the common open space for cooking, eating and parties. And when the home was ready, the wedding date would be set and preparations begun. The bride would never know the exact day or hour of the wedding, though she could guess on its approach, as her virgin friends gathered around her, waiting in their best clothes. Each would have been called by the bride's family, who would know the day at least.

Jesus laughed with the children and stood moving out into the crowd, the children surrounding. Holding in his hands two of the children, he continued. "In the months before, this young lover had worked hard in his field, clearing stones, tilling the soil, selecting only the best vines for planting. He did not allow his many hired servants to assist, for this field was his gift for his beloved." Looking back and up towards the Holy Place, he continued. "In the middle of his field he built a watchtower, beautiful and strong. All who came near wondered if it were not a temple, instead of a simple place of harvest. In it he carved out a wine press and waited for the harvest."

Turning again to the crowd and walking still further he continued. "On the day of celebration, all gathered for the days of festivity. Following the ceremony when all the guests had gathered in the family court yard to celebrate, the wine from his beloved's vineyard was brought out. Each guest received a generous cup of wine for the cup of honor, the toast offered by the groom to his beloved. And so, after taking the first drink, as a sign of his own covenant with his beloved, he drank and deeply. His eyes widened in horror as he choked and spit out the wine. Instead of it being sweet to the taste it was horribly bitter." The children were surprised at the outcome of Jeshua's story, as were we all. Jesus motioned them to be seated where they were. Then Jeshua slowly turned, making contact with everyone present, his voice growing more grave as he continued. Speaking in a loud voice he said, "Now, you people of Jerusalem and Judah, know this. Your lover is my Papa, in heaven. How he has longed to love you as a groom does his bride. How long he has waited for the day of wedding to come. But now, the wine has turned bitter in his mouth. Tell me, *what more could I have done for my beloved? When I expected sweet grapes, why did my vineyard give me bitter grapes?*

Suddenly I became aware that Jesus was quoting the prophet Isaiah in the Song of the Vineyard. Turning away from the crowd and toward the officials gathered on the edges he continued in a loud voice, speaking first person and no longer as one telling a story. *"Now let me tell you what I will do to my vineyard: I will tear down its hedges and let it be destroyed. I will break down its walls and let the animals trample it. I will make it a wild place where the vines are not pruned and the ground is not hoed, a place overgrown with briers and thorns. I will command the clouds to drop no rain on it"* (Isaiah 5: 4-6). Then, once again gathering a child into his arms and motioning the others to follow he started back to the steps of the Holy Place and continued, softer in tone. "The nation of Israel is the vineyard of the LORD of heaven's Armies. The people of Judah are his pleasant garden. He expected a crop of justice, but instead he found oppression. He expected to find righteousness, but instead he heard cries of violence." Taking his seat once more, almost as an afterthought, he added. "Still, I will drink the cup of bitter wine, until it is all gone. All of it."

It was at that very moment that some of the Temple elders chose to challenge him. *"By what authority,"* they said, *"are you doing* all *these things?"*(Luke 20:2)

What caught my attention, however, was not Jeshua's response, for I had just noticed Mary, the mother of our Lord, making her way under the portico and into the Court of Women.

Reflections on "Bitter Wine"

So much of life is filled with joy, followed by tragedy. This scene in the Holy Temple is the epitome of both.

Q: How does Jesus life, words, passion, death and resurrection give new context in the reading of the Old Testament's story of God's passionate love and anger towards Israel?

Q: Is the Church of Jesus Christ a wine sweet or bitter? ...which are you?

Consider the willingness of Jesus (thus the Father—Spirit) to drink the wine, though bitter... Pray for your church and yourself:

Week-7: WEDNESDAY—Matthew 6: 10 & Isaiah 4: 2-6 & Mark 4: 30-32 & 11: 12-14, 20-25 & John 15: 1-2

Story 29—The Trees

The day had begun, as the last two had on the Mount of Olives, at the crest of the hill before the road goes down into the Kidron Valley, near Gethsemane's gardens and up to the Temple mount. We had spent the evening at Simeon's home in Bethany and then retired at Lazarus and Martha and Mary's home.

Jeshua had just passed the fig tree that he had cursed yesterday. The fig tree represented Israel's promise of bearing fruit for Yahweh, of feeding the whole world with news of God's faithful and holy love.

Reaching the crest of Mt. Olives, Jeshua stopped and turned to his left, looking directly at the Herodian in the distance. He was now standing under a Mustard tree and so reached up to pull some developing mustard seeds, the smallest of all seeds in Israel. The Herodian was built by Herod the Great, a fortress built inside of a mountain. This fortress was where Herod would run if disaster came upon him from Rome, because of any miscalculation in his policy of appeasing the Emperor.

The Herodian

I was standing beside the Master. Peter was still at some distance back, gazing upon the fig tree Jeshua had cursed the day before. Peter had noticed that the sprouting figs, not yet mature, had changed and were now showing signs of disease. *"Rabbi,"* he called out, *"Look! The fig tree you cursed has withered!"* Jesus just smiled. He did not look back at Peter but kept staring at the hill called Herodian.

"Peter," he responded, still facing south and west but now looking down at the Mustard seeds in his hands. "Peter, I have often told you if you had only the faith of a mustard seed, you could say to this mountain…" He was now lifting his hand toward the Herodian, the mustard seeds falling to the ground. The rest of the disciples, including Peter, were gathering near him to hear. "…To this mountain, *'Go, throw yourself into the sea,' and does not doubt…"* Now Jeshua turned looking directly at Peter, "in his heart *but believes that what he says will happen, it will be done for him."* Turning to all of us, he continued. *"Whatever you ask for in prayer, believe that you have received it, and it will be yours."* Then Jeshua moved toward Judas Iscariot and placing his hand on his shoulder continued. "I tell you all plainly. Do not doubt the power of my love. For *when you stand praying, if you hold anything against anyone, forgive him, so that your Father in heaven may forgive you your sins"* (Mark 11: 21-25). He then turned and made his way to the Temple Mount for the day's teachings.

Reflections on "The Trees"

The story of the fig tree provides insight into the emotions of Jesus that last week. A man under incredible pressure, he closed his days in love. Still, this story reveals something of the bitterness which must have been felt by Jesus, emotionally.

On his first or second day in Jerusalem, he goes up to a fig tree and takes a bite of the fig, hoping for the pleasure of comforting taste. He is given none because the fruit had not matured. So he curses the tree. Zaps it apparently, as only the Creator and Lord can. What makes the story even more pregnant with irony, is that the tree should not have yet been ripe. Jesus would have surely known that.

Still, in all, he did not take out on any human being his bitter feelings of betrayal by Judas and rejection by the elders and the lesser feeling of being abandoned by his own.

Q: How does Jesus life, words, passion, death and resurrection give new context to your own emotional/spiritual struggles?

Consider the most difficult season in your life's journey in light of Jesus response to his own.

Turn your past or present into a prayer of confession, petition or thanksgiving.

Week-7: THURSDAY—MATTHEW 5: 43-45 & MARK 14: 1-11 & JOHN 13: 1-16

MY THOUGHTS 15—ENEMIES END

"The full implications of this call to love are hard to grasp. The kind of love Jesus calls us to includes the enemy, not just the friendly neighbor. Such love may in many ways run counter to our desires, needs, or expectations. Our understanding of love is so strongly influenced by ideas from interpersonal human relationships—personal attraction, mutual compatibility, sexual desires, cultural understandings of sensitivity—that we have trouble realizing that the love of God goes far beyond these...

Thus there seems to be a long chain of interlocking wounds and needs that stretch back into the long past and forward into our future. This picture drives us to turn love into a kind of mechanical exchange: "I will love you if you love me; I will give to you if you give to me; I will lend to you if you give me the same amount."

From "Turning My Mourning into Dancing by Henri Nouwen, "The End of Enemies," Page #86-88.

"Father, forgive them, for they do not know what they are doing" (Luke 23: 34). These were the final words of reconciliation offered by Jesus to his enemies. It was in the form of a prayer. It was a gift of forgiveness, releasing from judgment; His judgment and his Father's.

These words also echo through the centuries, before and after the Christ event (life, passion, death, resurrection, words). These words come down to you and me and from us to those who have wounded us. It is a universal as well as deeply personal statement. And they came from one who allowed his enemy to be near to him, even to the end, Judas Iscariot.

Reflections on "Enemies end"

Q: Have you received into yourself the release from judgment Jesus gave you, at the cross?

Q: In like manner, can you release into the Father's holy—love those who wound you?

Take some moments and create an 'enemies list'... Consider tearing it up once and for all time... and eternity!

Week-7: FRIDAY—MATTHEW 6: 9-13 & LUKE 22: 7-23 & JOHN 13: 16-38 & 14: 1-6

STORY 30—THE CUP

Lifting the fourth cup of the Passover, Jeshua gave thanks. "Blessed are You, O LORD, King of the universe, who gives us the fruit of the vine." Then looking around at each, his eyes tender and with a touch of sadness, said. *"I will not drink again of the fruit of the vine until the Kingdom of my Father comes in fullness"* (Luke 22: 18). I had been leaning sideways to Jeshua, against his shoulder, facing Peter. Now I turned. My attention quickened. Jeshua continued. *"My children, I will be with you only a little longer. You will look for me, and just as I told our brethren in the Temple, so I tell you now. "Where I am going, you cannot come"* (John 13: 33).

'What is he saying?' I wondered. Looking away and down, staring into my cup of wine, Jeshua's words began to fade. In their place his last words in the Temple, the day before, came thundering back. With great passion he had said to the chief priests, elders of the people, and all gathered. "You will not see me again until I come to receive from my Father the Kingdom prepared for me since before the world began. On that day, you will learn to cry out, 'Blessed is He who comes in the Name of the LORD!" With that he turned and we followed. All but Judas Iscariot, that is. He caught up with us later.

This day had begun with a sense of joy, even peace. It was a welcome contrast to the last few days. The sun was bright and a gentle breeze surrounded as Peter and I had made our way into Jerusalem from Bethany with instructions to prepare for the Passover. The other eleven and Jeshua were evidently taking the day off and resting at Lazarus home. Peter and I were chattering away about the week's events, when coming upon the Dung Gate, we noticed him. As Jeshua had said, he would be there carrying a heavy jug of water for his household. That meant that the household was very wealthy, for in poor houses it would be the women who would do the work of carrying the water. We soon learned that he was the servant of Clopas and Mary, the uncle and aunt of Jeshua. Their home was spacious with a large upper room, perfect for such a gathering.

Passover was my favorite of all the festivals. It was the heart of our Story. The week's tensions seemed to melt in the expectation of celebrating our people's deliverance from Egyptian bondage. We were making the last of the preparations when the others barged in upon us, saying nothing. Their silence betrayed an anger threatening the joy of the evenings rituals. My brother James caught my attention and warned me that once again the bantering about who would have what ministries in Jeshua's kingdom, at first harmless, had turned to hurt and hurt to anger and anger to silence.

I chose to gently engage my silent brothers, ignoring their feelings of distance. Soon the atmosphere of the room had warmed all of our hearts and all was forgotten. Peter and I also forgot our manners. As hosts, it was our duty to wash our brother's feet, especially the Rabbi's. We sang some hymns. After I had returned from taking the ritual water for cleansing of the hands around to each person, Jeshua, turning and placing his hand upon my forearm simply said, "Allow me." And taking the water basin and a towel he began to wash our feet as well. Peter and I were deeply ashamed at our failure to offer this courtesy, but the humility of his service was a profound gift, not unlike the gift Mary had given the night before at Simeon's. In this simple act and his teaching, he had addressed the growing contention among us. Then came the first cup and our Master's blessings, the meal and the unfolding ritual of Passover.

"I am telling you now before it happens." 'What happens?' My thoughts were suddenly refocused upon Jeshua and the unfolding sadness that was even now pouring in upon us. "I tell you the truth," Jeshua hesitated, looking first at me, then Peter and then around the room. *"One of you is going to betray me"* (John 13: 19a, 21b). Again, I looked down, in shock. Peter, who was seated to my right, leaned in and quietly insisted. "John, ask him who it is?" The others were looking at each other, some beginning to ask Jeshua if they were possibly capable of such an act. Without thinking, almost as a child's response to his mother, I leaned sideways and back into Jeshua's shoulder. "Master, who is it? Who could possibly…?"

Peter broke into our doubts and questions of possible guilt and standing, declared his own certainty. "Master!" he said, turning straight to Jesus. I kept my head and body leaning into the master, somehow taken in by the cup before Jeshua, now ready for its fourth filling. "Master!" I heard Peter repeat. "Even if all fall away, I will not!"

Jesus simply ignored him for a moment and Peter, feeling a little exposed, sat down somewhat awkwardly. I could imagine his eyes looking back and forth to assess the moment, but I did not turn away from Jeshua. I felt as though I were being protected like a little boy in his mother's arms. Slowly, those gathered around began to talk among themselves. The questions of tender vulnerability, "Lord, is it I?" slowly turned into challenges. "Who could do such a thing?" I think it was Philip who raised the question above a whisper.

Looking ahead of me, to Jeshua's left was Judas Iscariot. Jeshua had given him the seat of honor on this evening. He seemed withdrawn into himself, simply eating, his eyes looking up and around, ill at ease. Jeshua spoke to me in a whisper. "John, *it is the one to whom I will give this piece of bread when I have dipped it in the dish"* (John 13:26). Then taking the bread and dipping it, he handed it to Judas. My heart sank. But what overwhelmed me was the tender love of Jeshua's next statement to Judas Iscariot. "Judas, if you must do it, get it done and over with. Now." Judas looked up into Jeshua's eyes and then glanced down at me. For a moment, I think he wondered if Jeshua knew what was in his heart and approved. Jeshua simply added, "Go." And Judas left, taking his secret with him. He was neither embarrassed by Jesus, nor mentioned again. I sat up and watched as Judas left. I knew that somehow he too was acting out of conviction, though blinded by his lack of faith in Jesus.

"Peter," Jeshua began, now loud enough for all to hear. *"Will you really lay down your life for me?"* And now taking the fourth and final cup he looked straight into Peter's eyes as he poured the wine. "Peter, *I tell you* the truth, *before the rooster crows, you will disown me three times!"* (John 13:38) I glanced at Peter, as we all did. His eyes looked as if he had been the one betrayed.

Then standing and taking the fourth cup with him, Jeshua spoke with a deep and tender authority. *"Do not let your hearts be troubled,"* he began moving around the room. "In my Father's house are many rooms." He was now lifting the cup in the direction of Clopas beautiful upper chamber to illustrate. *"If that were not so, I would have told you."* Turning again to us, he continued. *"I am going there to prepare a place for you. And if I go and prepare a place for you, I will come back and take you to be with me that you also may be where I am"* (John 14: 1,2). 'Is this what I think it is?' I wondered. Jeshua seemed to be introducing into the Passover the cup of the groom before his bride.

You see, at the final negotiations between a groom, his papa and the potential bride and her papa, this is exactly the promise given. After the price is negotiated and it would be expensive, the groom would raise his cup to the bride. In that act he would be saying, "all that I have and am is yours, for life". Then he would give the bride his cup. If she drank from it she was saying in effect, "...and all that I am is now yours." Then the groom would leave to his papa's villa, an open compound for the extended family, around which all the homes or rooms of the extended family would be built. In that open courtyard all the life of the family would be celebrated. The groom would work for the next months or year building his own home or room for he and his bride to be. As the wedding day approached only the bride would not know the day of the wedding, though she might guess at it in the increasing presence of her virgin friends as they waited the trumpeted processional of the groom and his friends that would suddenly come upon her, perhaps as a surprise. Then they would all return to the groom's villa and begin the wedding rituals, all begun in the cup.

Suddenly, my mind raced to the teachings in the temple this week. Jesus had emphasized those parables which hinted at this very ritual, common to every Jewish and Samaritan village throughout Judea, Samaria and Galilee. Jeshua had walked around the whole room and was now taking his seat, when he lifted the cup and said. "This fourth cup, which is the sign of my Papa's faithful love to Israel is now to be the cup of promise that my Papa and I make to you, to the whole world." My heart quickened within 'like a bride would before her groom.' I smiled, at the thought. "This cup," Jeshua continued "is sealed by my own blood, shed for the forgiveness of sin for all who will drink." Then he drank from it, himself. "All that I am, I give to you." And he added, "As often as you drink, do so in remembrance of me. For I and my Father are coming to you."

Then Jeshua, having turned the Passover Meal into betrothal covenant, gave the cup to me. He asked, "Will you drink, also?" In that moment I knew only one thing. I loved him. And I passed the cup on to Peter.

Reflections on "The Cup"

Q: How does this imaginative retelling of that night affect your thoughts and feelings about:
- Peter
- Jesus
- John
- Judas Iscariot

Q: How does the relation of 'The Cup of Holy Communion' and the 'Cup of Betrothal' change, deepen or muddy your own experience of Holy Communion?

The next opportunity you have to receive The Cup allow Jesus to say "All I am and have I give to you" and allow yourself to respond in kind or confess the desire to do so—for now, go & pray.

Week-7: SATURDAY—MATTHEW 5: 5 & 7: 7 & ZECHARIAH 13: 7 & JOHN 14: 30, 31 & 15: 1-4 & MARK 14: 32-42 & JOHN 17: 1-7,16-23

STORY 31—WILL YOU DRINK ALSO?

Most of the journey from the upper room to Gethsemane had been in silence. A heavy cloud had descended upon the eleven of us who had left everything to follow the One who apparently was about to leave us. Passing near the Temple, Jesus looked up and noticed in the moon light the sculpturing of a large grape vine on the wall. He had stopped, looked at the sign of Israel, as though in a distant gaze and then turned with a gentle smile.

"I am the true vine, and my Father is the gardener. He cuts off every branch in me that bears no fruit, while every branch that does bear fruit he prunes so that it will be even more fruitful" (John 15: 1,2).

For a moment we forgot the myriad of emotions that had surrounded the Passover meal and had taken rest in the gentle teaching of our master. Jeshua spoke with us as friends, taking us into his confidence, telling us the secrets of his love. Then, he stood and walked in silence once again, down the hillside, below the Temple and out into the Kidron Valley. The mood dampened under the shadows of the moon spilling out into the grove of trees that surrounded our path. Just outside of Gethsemane, near a gentle creek, Jesus stopped. His shoulders stooped and in sorrow, matching our own, declared. *"Now I am going to him who sent me"* (John 16: 5). We had stopped asking him "where" he was going. We no longer cared, lost as we were to anything but our dulled depression.

Jesus reached out and placed his hand on my shoulder and continued. *"I tell you the truth: It is for your good that I am going away. Unless I go away, the Counselor will not come to you"* (John 16:7). Jeshua told us that his Papa had given into Jesus hands, all things. He seemed to believe that his leaving would somehow make the Father available to us, in us; I'm not sure what he meant. I only know how tired I felt and how I very much wanted to run away from the approaching shadows.

Jesus sat down for just a moment to rest. The gate into Gethsemane was now in view. This familiar garden was a welcome sight. At least we could get some sleep. *"In a little while,"* the master continued, *"you will see me no more, and then after a little while you will see me..."* He hesitated. *"...because I am going to the Father."* The thought crossed my own mind that perhaps Jesus was losing it. 'Perhaps Judas is right, after all.' I shook the thought away. Jesus, looking up from the ground continued. *"Now is your time of grief, but I will see you again and you will rejoice"* (John 16: 16,22). The joy he seemed to refer to would rest in our ability to approach His Father in prayer, just like Jesus. He even spoke of His Father being moved by our prayers because of His love for us and our love for Jesus. Looking straight into my eyes, Jesus said, *"The Father himself loves you because you have loved me and have believed that I came from God. I came from the Father and entered the world; now I am leaving the world and going back to the Father"* (John 16: 27,27).

I walked over and stood just above my friend. "Lord," I said, hesitantly, "we know you speak only what God tells you to say." At that, Jesus stood and walked around and between each of us, slowly, purposefully and began to pray, as only he could; Son to Father, friend with friend, companion with companion.

Then Jeshua led us through the gate into the garden. The deepening shadows seemed welcoming. Most of us bedded down for the night in the shadows. Motioning to me and then Peter and James, Jeshua led us still further in. We sat down against an old and giant olive tree for rest and hopefully some sleep. Jeshua knelt before us, the silver light of the moon crossing his forehead. For moment his hair glistened as if a halo surrounded. "Peter, John, James; watch with me. *I am filled with sorrow, to the point of death"* (Mark 14: 34). And so we settled in to watch with him. Jeshua went deeper still into an open space with the moon's light forming a kind of pillow. He knelt beside a large rock and began to pray.

I began to pray, but my eyes grew tired. My body longed for sleep, though my soul wanted to wait with my Master, to keep him company. I tried to listen. Jeshua's prayer sounded like a human whispering, murmuring, the rhythm, like that of a kitten purring. I could not make out his words, only the pattern of them. My eyes were closing. 'John! Stay awake!' My heart's mind was screaming within. Suddenly, I heard the cry of Jeshua's soul. He pleaded, his voice a dark whisper. "Papa!" he cried, 'Take this cup from me!" My eyes opened. I turned my head and noticed Jeshua laying prostrate on the ground. "Take this cup!" he repeated. "Nevertheless...," and I could not make out the rest of words. The rhythm of an intense murmur again became the pattern. My eyes slowly drifted shut.

Years later the whole of Jeshua's prayer for us, just outside of Gethsemane's gates, would pour out from my heart's memory. In time, I would see the irony of Jeshua's spirit being crushed in a garden whose very name was Gethsemane, referring to the mill stones used to crush olives in the region of Galilee. And only days later I would find the courage to ask my Master the nature of his passionate prayer, alone in the garden. But that night I knew only one thing. On the night in which Jeshua needed me to drink of his cup, I fell asleep.

Note: Context taken from Michael Card's "The Parable of Joy", Chapter 16

Reflections on "Will You Drink Also?"

Going into the garden that night was 13 lonely men. Jesus and 11 disciples and one betrayer.

Q: With whom do you identify? ...Why?
- Jesus
- John, Peter, James
- Judas Iscariot
- The other eight disciples?

Q: What is the relation between exhaustion and sin? ...Is it really an issue of the heart, always? ...How so? ...Why not?

Consider the relationship between sleep, depression and vulnerable spaces in your life... and offer to God all those places.

Week-7: SUNDAY—MATTHEW 5: 17-18 & PSALM 22: 1-19 & ZECHARIAH 12: 10 & 13: 1 & JOHN 18: 12-14, 19-24, 28 & 19: 16-42 & MATTHEW 26: 57-64

STORY 32—POURED OUT

"Mary, wake up! Your son..." Mary's eyes were instantly alert. "John, what's the matter?" Without explanation, I simply commanded. "Get dressed. I will take you to him." It was the fourth watch of the night, about four a.m. as we made our way to the High Priest's home. It was only a guess, but I had told Peter to wait for me there while I went to get Jeshua's mother.

As we approached the gated home I caught a glimpse of Peter standing in the shadows. I motioned him to wait and escorted Mary toward the gate and the Temple guards who stood at attention. Looking in, I knew I had guessed well. The open courtyard before us was alive with activity including soldiers and servants standing around an open fire. "This is the mother of the prisoner brought before the elders tonight. Jesus of Galilee." I spoke with authority, hoping to cover my fear. "She is the niece of Zechariah, may Yahweh bless his memory and a friend of Joseph of Arimathea." I was hoping that we could bluff our way in. I did not need to, for from in front of us and behind the guard came a voice. "Open the gate! Welcome, Mary." It was Nicodemus and next to him stood Joseph. Quickly, I turned and motioned Peter to join us, advising the guard. "He is with us." We were in.

Joseph of Arimathea took charge and led us, Mary and I, beyond the courtyard and into the receiving room of the High

Priest's home. Peter motioned that he would remain in the outer court. His eyes were filled with fear, so I did not challenge, thinking it might be easier for him there.

Once inside, Joseph turned to us, speaking quietly. "Mary, I am so sorry, ashamed indeed, that a son of Israel, your son, would be treated as a common criminal and in the shadows, like this!" I could see that his eyes meant every word. He directed us to stand in the corner of the room, out of the way. "We, Nicodemus and I, will do all that we can for him." Mary said nothing, but acknowledged with a nod her appreciation. Nicodemus and Joseph turned to leave, but Mary reached out for Nicodemus arm. He turned and she spoke, for the first time. "Nicodemus, God's will be done." Nicodemus hesitated, taking in the peace of her countenance and then smiling, turned to join his friend.

Joseph and Nicodemus, together with one or two others challenged the proceeding itself. After the initial questioning by Annas, the administrator of the Sanhedrin, Jesus was ordered into the inner meeting room where most of the Sanhedrin had been gathering, waiting for Caiaphas, the son in law of Annas, whom he had appointed as the High Priest for that year. Jesus was still bound as Caiaphas entered.

The receiving room and the meeting room were open to each other with only colonnades separating, so we were able to witness the proceedings, together with a handful of servants, I assumed. One of the guards had already beaten Jeshua in the face. I felt Mary's body tremble as I held her close, as one does his mother in the face of tragedy.

I do not know how Mary was able to witness the proceedings. From the beginning it seemed unseemly, but now it was apparent to all that it was also contrived. Most of the time Jeshua remained silent, insisting that he had spoken openly in the Temple and before the people. *"Why question me? Ask those who heard me. Surely they know what I said"* (John 18: 21). But they didn't know. The testimony given was false and inconsistent. 'If this were a fair trial,' I thought, 'they would release him.' Apparently feeling the same, Nicodemus stood. He began slowly. All present clearly respected him. Hope began to rise within me. Again, he challenged the appropriateness of the proceedings and the hour, but quickly moved on to challenge the obvious. "Even the witnesses could not agree!" he said. Then Caiaphas stood, his hand extended to Nicodemus, palm up, as though agreeing. "Nicodemus," he began, "you are wise and your counsel is always heeded by this great assembly. But there is only one question today of which we have concern." And then, turning to Jeshua he asked. "Are you or are you not the Messiah of Israel, the Son of the living God?"

Mary raised her hand to her heart. You could almost hear a community gasp. Caiaphas had cut to the central issue and Jeshua's fate was now clearly in his own hand. Jesus, for the first time, in the High Priest's presence, looked up and into his eyes. *"I Am"* he said. Now the gasp, previously felt became audible. *"And,"* Jeshua continued. *"You will see the Son of Man sitting at the right hand of the Mighty One and coming on the clouds of heaven."* With that the High Priest tore his clothes, from top to bottom, declaring, *"Why do we need any more witnesses? You have heard the blasphemy"* (Mark 14: 62, 63). Nicodemus simply sat down. I tightened my grip around Mary's waist.

The rest of the day began to tumble forward following the sign of rejection, in the tearing of the clothes, by the High Priest of God Most High. Nicodemus and Joseph ushered us back out and beyond the gate of Caiaphas home. They said little, but you could feel the horror that was still apparent in their eyes, as they left us to shadow the events of the day, now unfolding. They had promised to do what they could. 'But what could they do?' I wondered.

Peter was gone when we came out. Mary wanted to follow. A crowd was now gathering and so we blended in. Standing with the crowd in the open court of the Procurator, Pontius Pilate, we could only guess at what was happening. At mid-morning, we learned that Jeshua was to be taken before Herod Antipas, who was in Jerusalem for the Festival. Mary wanted to follow. For the first time, I took control. "Mary, he will be taken back to Pilate's palace eventually. Herod has no authority. You will need strength for the day. Come, we will go to an open street café, near this court." Mary relented and we made our way.

After a quiet lunch, I found a place where we could sit, Mary leaning against my breast, as I had her son only hours before. We slept and deeply. I do not know how, though it was a grace. It was early afternoon, when we awakened to the cries of "Crucify Him! Crucify Him!" Mary looked up and into my face. Quickly we gathered our belongings and walked back to Pilate's courtyard. We entered under the portico when silence ensued. Looking up, I saw Pilate in his seat of judgment, hand raised. "Would you have me crucify your King?" Mary stopped suddenly, taking in the question. In the distance we could make out Caiaphas voice with clarity. *"We have no king but Caesar!"* (John 19: 15) I could not believe what I was hearing? 'Blasphemy?' I thought. But the sounds of "Crucify Him!" again filled the moment.

I placed my arm around Mary and began to pull her from the scene. For the first time, she did not object. She was mumbling something. Only later, as we walked down the Via Della Rosa did I hear her murmuring prayer, above the echoes of the crowd, now fading in the distance. "Your will, be done." She repeated over and again.

I walked Mary toward the Damascus Gate and found a shaded area in which to wait. I realized within, that if crucifixion was to happen it would be on the Roman scaffolding beyond that gate.

"Why John, why?" I listened. "And where are the twelve,"? she finally asked as we waited, knowing now what seemed inevitable. I did not answer. I only held her. I had not yet told her of my betrayal in the garden and how I ran at his arrest. She did not need my confessions just then. The words of Jeshua, at Mt Hermon, continued to echo in my heart, even as they were now unfolding before me.

In about an hour we saw them coming up the narrow street. Just before the Gate the way opens up and turns, so we were able to catch a side view. In front were two Roman soldiers on horse, followed by a group of six soldiers on foot. Behind were three convicted as criminals and who carried their cross bars for crucifixion. Immediately behind was another contingent of Roman foot soldiers. Following was a crowd, some loud and accusing. *"He trusts in the Lord; let the LORD rescue him!"* (Psalm 22: 8a) they shouted. Others were crying, some just watching with interest at the show. At the rear were two more soldiers on horse.

As they passed near us, maybe twenty feet in distance, we had our first good look at Jeshua. Mary gasped. His body and face were covered in blood. He had clearly been beaten with open sores still flowing from his back. On his head was a twisted Roman crown, one given to sports heroes. However, this was made of the thorns of a grape vine and pressed into his skull, the two inch barbs still showing signs of fresh blood. He had been striped to his loin cloth, but surrounded with a purple sash, the kind worn by a king. Suddenly, just as Jeshua was passing he stumbled forward and fell to the ground, his cross bar falling down upon him and rolling over his thorny crown onto the ground in front.

The troop began to come into some disarray. The soldiers on horse, started barking out orders for all to stop and stand in place. Mary, jumped from my arms and ran to her son as only a mother can. The horseman seemed not to mind, as his initial focus was on crowd control. Now the soldiers at the front joined and were pointing to a man, we later would come to know as Simon, from Cyrene.

Jeshua began to pull himself up. Mary was helping him, leaning over him. Recognizing her, he reached out his hand to her cheek and simply said. "Woman, do not weep for me, but for the city." Then, slowly he stood erect, with Mary and my help. He looked around and in a loud voice cried out to those women who had been following, weeping and wailing as one does in a funeral procession. *"Daughters of*

Who Am I?

Jerusalem," he cried, "do not weep for me; weep for yourselves and for your children. For the time will come when you will say, 'Blessed are the barren women, the wombs that never bore and the breasts that never nursed!'" (Luke 23: 28)

I glanced up at the Roman soldiers on horseback, wondering when they would strike Jesus down. But they simply sat motionless, mesmerized, as did the other criminals and the crowd, now very large, in number. Jesus continued. *"Then they will say to the mountains, 'Fall on us!' and to the hills, 'Cover us!' For if men do these things when the tree is green, what will happen when it is dry"* (Luke 23: 30-31).

With that Jeshua turned back, facing forward. He had glanced over at Simon and smiled. 'How,' I wondered, 'could he love, even now.'

I pulled Mary, with some force, back out of the way. The Roman soldier, who had been at the front, took control and ordered everyone forward. It was then that I noticed Mary of Magdalene, in the crowd. We joined her and continued on with the troop.

We made our way to Golgotha, the place of the skull. As we approached, Nicodemus and Joseph of Arimathea joined. Their presence opened the way for Mary to gather in near the front. "She is his mother," Nicodemus had said to the commander.

All that followed became a blur of emotion, as the spikes were nailed into Jeshua's wrist against the cross beam. A small comfort was given in the rope that was tied around his arms, giving support as he was raised upon the scaffolding, the cross finally nailed into place. Then the last spike was nailed through his feet into the support rest below, so that he could periodically stand to catch his breath.

What captured my heart's memory was Jeshua and Mary. Jeshua, even in this moment remained focused on the needs of those around; To the criminal on his left he gave eternal comfort. To Joseph and Nicodemus, he simply said "thank you, my friends." He cared for his mother. "Dear woman," he said, referring to me, "here is your son". And to me he said, "Here is your mother" (John 19: 26b, 27a). Even his cry, "My God, why?" seemed more like the cry of a son seeking understanding than a challenge. To the soldiers and those who accused him falsely, he declared, "Father, forgive them. For they do not know what it is they are doing" (Luke 23: 34).

But the extraordinary moment came only at the end. Nearly all had left, frightened and driven away by the thunder, pouring rain and the earthquake accompanying his death. The Roman guards clearly wanted to bring this unusual crucifixion to an early end. Jeshua was apparently already dead and so, to be sure, they pierced his side. Water and blood flowed from his side like a gusher. Mary had approached now, unchallenged and taken her place at his feet sitting with her back to the scaffolding. As Jeshua was lowered, she reached up and gathered him in her arms as a mother gathers her new borne, wet with blood and water.

In that moment all was loss: blood and water mingling with the rainy mist pouring over us threatening to become the torrents of an angry storm. Even so, as I watched this powerful scene unfold—almost detached, perhaps in shock that night—I was taken back at the picture before me; The mother of my Lord holding in her lap, the son of the Living God.

It is a scene I've now had a life to reflect upon. Mary held Jeshua with such tender love as you would your favorite lamb. The rain never became more than a drizzle, like a mist washing over her and Jeshua; Isaiah's words capture the scene like a painting. *"Surely he took up our pain and bore our suffering, yet we considered him punished by God, stricken by him, and afflicted. But he was pierced for our transgressions, he was crushed for our iniquities; the punishment that brought us peace was on him, and by his wounds we are healed. We all, like sheep, have gone astray, each of us has turned to our own way; and the Lord has laid on him the iniquity of us all"* (Isaiah 53: 4-6). And John the Baptists proclamation that led me to leave him and follow Jeshua now echoes in my heart even today. "Behold, the Lamb of God who takes away the sin of the world."

Weeks later, it hit me as Jeshua's words on the cross filled my torn heart, even in the daze of that first night. "Father forgive." That surely includes me; even me and the whole world with me. And painted on the walls of my heart is the picture of all the sins of the world poured into his body, now being held by the very mother of God. The cup had been poured by Jeshua's Papa, in heaven.

Reflections on "Poured Out"

Your Reflections:

EPILOGUE—EASTER SUNDAY
...The Birth of The New Age

Story 33—Resurrection

The rest of the day had been spent in sorrow. Joseph of Arimathea, at great risk to his own place within the Sanhedrin, offered his own burial site near Golgotha. It was a small comfort to Mary that it had never been used and was expansive, dedicated to a prestigious member of the ruling council. We gathered the spices and linen cloths and placed him in the tomb.

Making our way to Mary's, the wife of Clopus, home, the mother of my Lord finally gave into her emotions and wept, deeply. It was the cry of the soul, heavy and billowing like the waves of Galilee in a tempestuous storm. We both did. I simply held her. We had found a quiet place near the south side of the Temple and sat for a rest. Then, after the release of emotion we continued our journey in silence. It was about midnight when at last we came home. I was not surprised to find my brother already there, together with most of the others. Only Peter had not showed. And Judas Iscariot of course.

On the evening of the second day Peter finally had made his way to the home, where it all began, in the upper room. The memory of that Passover night kept echoing against the walls of the cavern of my soul. I searched our celebration for some clue as to the purpose in his death. Jeshua had clearly known, since Mt. Herman, at least. '"Who do the people say I am? Who do you say I am?"' Who indeed? In the thick cloud that surrounded our silence, the eleven, Mary Magdalene, Mary the mother of my Lord, Mary and Clopus and John Mark, I wondered how any of us could go on, much less drink again of the cup Jeshua had offered. '"Will you drink also?"' He had said.

In the fog of my heart, in the depths of my soul I could find no emotion, no vision or rabbinic teaching that could awaken me to that memory; much less recreate the moment he offered us himself in the cup, as anything but betrayal. I had lost faith. 'Who are you, Jeshua?' I wondered to myself, afraid to declare my thoughts. 'Who were you?' I corrected myself. And then, I lay down to sleep. It was the sixth hour of a new day. Sunday morning.

It was surreal. I could not make out in the shadows of black and white if it was a dream or a vision. I could not even tell if I was asleep. But I knew that I was standing in a place in the distant past, before creation itself, perhaps tens of thousands of years, in human time. One whose features were surrounded in light, stood beside His Father. I thought, in my sleep or vision, 'I have seen this person before.' Then I remembered where. It was on the Mt. of Transfiguration. I was looking at Jeshua, before Jesus of Nazareth existed. Looking around I began to take in the scene. I was in the midst of beings of light, each with wings, six of them; Two above, two below and two in the middle. A thick darkness filled the place with the light of the Three at the center pouring into the darkness, providing illumination. 'Three?' I wondered at the sight. Yet before me, in the very center was One who was glory itself and to his right was Jeshua, before Jeshua, and surrounding was a cloud that you could see through, beautiful and filled with the colors of what I knew would become a rainbow. The colors seem to increase and decrease according to the rhythm of their conversation.

I suddenly felt the need to listen. I was not alone for the wings of the beings of light, angels I assumed, came to a quiet hum. Jeshua, before Jeshua and in communion with the Holy Cloud laughs! At what, I could not immediately tell. Then I saw it. I knew what it was. They were dreaming of the possibilities of 'water.' Out of their love, I can find no other word to describe the feeling; from deep within the Cloud whose brilliance radiated All LOVE a vision emerges of beings born from the water of life. It was then that I realized that I was witnessing the beginnings of Creation. Only later, from the water and born of a woman's labor a baby screams. "Yes, let us Create… Beings like us, yet different!"

Jeshua's eyes looked to the ONE in whom all glory lived and apparently from whom all final choices are made. "Father, please, let us expand our love to include a whole expanse filled with crystals of ice interacting with light and forming brilliant colors in the void, formless and empty. And so material light came into being exploding in brilliant shades of color as crystals of ice were shattered inside a thick void.

And the tens of thousands who watched and waited, who listened to the dreams of these Three whose love formed One; These who surround what appeared to be Father—Son—Cloud and who normally gave off a gentle flutter of wings, not unlike the purring of a kitten… These tens of thousands allowed their wings to become a thunderous applause at the appearance of material light like the crashing waters of a giant water fall! I clapped with them in delight.

Suddenly, as the Father lifts his hand, they stop, as One; a deep hush fills the expanse of nothing that has been shattered by light. All wait…and the Son waits…And the Cloud waits.

Who Am I?

A voice deeper than time forms The WORD. "If we give to beings other than us, this gift of creativity and choice, love will be shared as never before. But with this gift there may come a new birth of... (and I sensed The ONE hesitate at even the thought now forming) ...of un-love, now unreal but becoming real in hate and wounds and brokenness. On that day, should it come and one our created creatures turn from us, a price will have to be paid if love is to triumph over hate. The water will turn sour and have a salty taste."

The Holy One of Love, The Cloud groaned at the Words of the Father. This Holy Spirit could not understand what this word hate could possibly mean. The Colors of the Cloud or Spirit searched the heart of the Son and sensed the same uncertainty. And both turned to the Father.

Yet deep within the tens of thousands, hidden in the soul of one who looked on: One who was near me, who was an angel of beauty beyond all those gathered and One who knew choice, but not feeling—who understood adoration, but not love; Looking upon his face, I knew him.

How? I could not tell, but one thing I knew. I knew the look. It was the same look I had seen in Judas Iscariot and Peter and James and lived in me, I'm sure. In this beautiful angel was born the first spark of pride as he considered beings other than The Three whose love seemed to make them ONE, beings capable of—'what did the Father call it, love?' And in that moment evil was also born in the heart of one Lucifer.

"John! John! Wake up!" Slowly the vision or dream faded. I did not want it to. Not there. "John! Now!" The voice was urgent. Opening my eyes, I entered a world of living color. 'Awesome!' I thought. The color of the Spirit made real.' As I came to, the urgency of what was in her eyes focused my attention. "John!" she said one more time. "Yes, Mary, what?" Then Mary of Magdela responded. "You must come and Peter with you." Glancing over I saw that Peter was fully awake. "Why?" I asked. "The stone!" She was still exclaiming. "It has been moved. The stone over Jeshua's grave!" With that Peter ran out of the upper room and toward the door. I quickly put on my sandals and followed.

Reflections on "Resurrection"

The purpose of worship is to form in us, anew, the Story of God. Now, go, with John of old and live it out—the resurrection of Jesus Christ!

THE RE-BEGINNING!

Who Am I?

LENT RITE—ENTERING THE STORY
...A rite for Ash Wednesday

In our community we prepare our hearts on Ash Wednesday, to take the sign of the cross and begin a Lenten Season...

Alternate Rite: hold the rite of confession and the sign of the cross for Sunday morning. Then on Sunday, invite parishioners to come forward and form a line before one of your pastors, confessing (in private) a sin, wound or need. Prayer is then offered the parishioner, privately (in the presence of Christ's body) and he/she is given the sign of Lent, the cross...

Ash Wednesday Service

As our pastors pass the ash,
please touch and consider the cost to God
of our salvation...

Word of God Speak
Copy write rights at: CCLI Song # 3912788

I'm finding myself, At a loss for words,
And the funny thing is, it's okay.
The last thing I need,
Is to be heard, but to hear...
What You would say.

(chorus)
Word of God speak.
Would You pour down like rain,
Washing my eyes to see, Your majesty.
To be still and know,
That You're on this place.
Please let me stay and rest,
In Your holiness,
Word of God speak.

I'm finding myself, In the midst of You,
Beyond the music. Beyond the noise.
All that I need, Is to be with You,
And in the quiet, Hear Your voice.

(to Chorus)

Invocation

Visual
Dramatic Reading,
Brief Vignette (such as Mary washing Jesus feet) or Video focused on the last weeks of Christ's life, passion, burial...

Special
"Mary, Did you know?"

Scripture Reading
Matthew 16: 13-20

[13] When Jesus came to the region of Caesarea Philippi, he asked his disciples, "Who do people say the Son of Man is?" [14] They replied, "Some say John the Baptist; others say Elijah; and still others, Jeremiah or one of the prophets." [15] "But what about you?" he asked. "Who do you say I am?" [16] Simon Peter answered, "You are the Christ, the Son of the living God." [17] Jesus replied, "Blessed are you, Simon son of Jonah, for this was not revealed to you by man, but by my Father in heaven. [18] And I tell you that you are Peter, and on this rock I will build my church, and the gates of Hades will not overcome it. [19] I will give you the keys of the kingdom of heaven; whatever you bind on earth will be bound in heaven, and whatever you loose on earth will be loosed in heaven." [20] Then he warned his disciples not to tell anyone that he was the Christ.

Devotional

Why we take this Journey

The Holy Season of Lent

The reason for entering this season with attention is so that We, together, may walk with Jesus in his sorrow. Our purpose is to identify with his sufferings, as the Apostle Paul admonished us, "to know Christ and the power of his resurrection and the fellowship of sharing in his sufferings, becoming like him in his death, and so, somehow, to attain to the resurrection from the dead" (Phil 3: 10-11).

Scripture tells us to 'put off the old self' and to 'clothe ourselves in Christ'. We are called to be "given over to death for Jesus' sake, so that his life may be revealed in our mortal body" (II Cor. 11). This is fulfilled in us by the Holy Spirit, who is love, as He leads us into sacrificial giving.

So, in the Holy Season, we invite you to consider two questions:

- In your life, who is Christ, really?

- Is his life, death, passion and resurrection alive in you?

Hymn of Confession

Lord Have Mercy

Copy write rights at: CCLI Song # 2989578

Verses–Soloist
Chorus–Congregation Joins

Verse 1
Jesus I've forgotten
The words that You have spoken
Promises that burned within my heart
Have now grown dim
With a doubting heart I follow
The paths of earthly wisdom
Forgive me for my unbelief
Renew the fire again

Chorus
Lord have mercy
Christ have mercy
Lord have mercy on me
Lord have mercy
Christ have mercy
Lord have mercy on me

Verse 2
I have built an altar
Where I've worshipped things of man
I have taken journeys
That have drawn me far from You
Now I am returning
To Your mercies ever flowing
Pardon my transgressions
Help me love You again

(To Chorus)

Verse 3
I have longed to know You
And all Your tender mercies
Like a river of forgiveness
Ever flowing without end
So I bow my heart before You
In the goodness of Your presence
Your grace forever shining
Like a beacon in the night

(To Chorus)

Prayer of Confession and Repentance
from the Book of Common Worship & Psalms 51

Ldr: Let us pray.

Cong: **Have mercy on us, O God, according to Your loving-kindness; in Your great compassion blot out our offenses.**

Ldr: We have not loved you with our whole heart, and mind, and strength. We have not loved our neighbors as ourselves. We have not forgiven others as we have been forgiven.

Cong: **Wash us through and through from our wickedness and cleanse us from our sin.**

Ldr: We have not listened to your call to serve as Christ served us. We have not been true to the mind of Christ. We have grieved your Holy Spirit.

Cong: **Against You only, have we sinned and done what is evil in Your sight.**

Ldr: We confess to you, the pride, hypocrisy, and impatience in our lives.

Cong: **Indeed, we have been wicked from our birth, a sinner from our mother's womb.**

Ldr: Our self-indulgent appetites and ways and our exploitation of other people, Our frustration with our own failures and our envy of those more fortunate than ourselves.

Cong: **Purge us from our sin, and we shall be pure; wash us and we shall be clean.**

Ldr: Our love of worldly goods and comforts, and our dishonesty in daily life and work.

Cong: **Hide Your face from our sins and blot our all our iniquities.**

Ldr: For our negligence in prayer and worship, and our failure to witness to others the faith that is in us.

Cong: **Create in us a clean heart, O God, and renew a right spirit within us.**

Ldr: Accept our repentance, O God, in the wrongs we have done and for what we have left undone. For our neglect of human need and suffering and our indifference to injustice and cruelty.

Cong: **Cast us not away from Your presence and take not Your Holy Spirit from us.**

Ldr: For all our judgments and uncharitable thoughts toward our neighbors, and for our prejudice and contempt toward those who differ from us.

Cong: **Give us the joy of Your saving help again and sustain us with Your bountiful Spirit.**

Ldr: Restore us, O God, and let your anger depart from us and love form in us, Christ.

Cong: **Then we shall teach Your ways to the wicked, and sinners shall return to You.**

Ldr: The sacrifice of God is a troubled spirit; a broken and contrite heart, O God You will not despise.

Cong: **Amen.**

Who Am I?

Hymn of Adoration

The Wondrous Cross

Copy write rights at: CCLI Song # 3148435

Verse 1
When I survey the wondrous cross
On which the Prince of Glory died
My richest gain I count but loss
And pour contempt on all my pride

Verse 2
See from His Head His Hands His feet
Sorrow and love flow mingled down
Did e'er such love and sorrow meet
Or thorns compose so rich a crown

Chorus 1
O the wonderful cross
O the wonderful cross
Bids me come and die and find
That I may truly live
O the wonderful cross
O the wonderful cross
All who gather here by grace
Draw near and bless Your name

Verse 3
Were the whole realm of nature mine
That were an offering far too small
Love so amazing so divine
Demands my soul my life my all

Rev. Terry Mattson

Scripture Reading

Philippians 2: 1-13

Imitating Christ's Humility

[1] If you have any encouragement from being united with Christ, if any comfort from his love, if any fellowship with the Spirit, if any tenderness and compassion, [2] then make my joy complete by being likeminded, having the same love, being one in spirit and purpose. [3] Do nothing out of selfish ambition or vain conceit, but in humility consider others better than yourselves. [4] Each of you should look not only to your own interests, but also to the interests of others. [5] Your attitude should be the same as that of Christ Jesus: [6] Who, being in very nature God, did not consider equality with God something to be grasped, [7] but made himself nothing, taking the very nature of a servant, being made in human likeness. [8] And being found in appearance as a man, he humbled himself and became obedient to death—even death on a cross! [9] Therefore God exalted him to the highest place and gave him the name that is above every name, [10] that at the name of Jesus every knee should bow, in heaven and on earth and under the earth, [11] and every tongue confess that Jesus Christ is Lord, to the glory of God the Father. [12] Therefore, my dear friends, as you have always obeyed—not only in my presence, but now much more in my absence—continue to work out your salvation with fear and trembling, [13] for it is God who works in you to will and to act according to his good purpose.

Visual
Dramatic Reading,
Brief Vignette (such as Mary washing Jesus feet) or Video focused on the last weeks of Christ's life, passion, burial...

Hymn of Affirmation

How Deep the Father's Love for Us

Copy write rights at: CCLI Song # 1558110

Verse 1
How deep the Father's love for us
How vast beyond all measure
That He should give His Only Son
To make a wretch His treasure
How great the pain of searing loss
The Father turns His face away
As wounds which mar the Chosen One
Bring many sons to glory

Verse 2
Behold the Man upon a cross
My sin upon His shoulders
Ashamed I hear my mocking voice
Call out among the scoffers
It was my sin that held Him there
Until it was accomplished
His dying breath has brought me life
I know that it is finished

Verse 3
I will not boast in anything
No gifts no pow'r no wisdom
But I will boast in Jesus Christ
His death and resurrection
Why should I gain from His reward
I cannot give an answer
But this I know with all my heart
His wounds have paid my ransom

Confessional Silence

With classical style or non-descript emotive music playing allow your parishioners the opportunity of two-three minutes of quiet reflection and writing out their confession of sin or wound or need.

Instructions: Write a prayer to God or from God to you… Focus on the wounds, sins and life experiences that need to be fully surrendered to God, if you wish to follow Jesus of Nazareth, to walk in his steps…

Illustrated soft visual for writing of confessions
THE ARK AND MERCY SEAT.

Then invite your parishioners forward to receive the sign of the cross and proceed outside to burn these confessions also in silence, perhaps closing with "Amazing Grace" or "I Love You Lord" (some spiritual song or hymn well known).

Note: Keep the ashes for the next year's sign of the cross.

On Sunday: Open a time for confessional prayer in support of Wednesday's confession and commitment to Lent.

Alternate Rite: We have at times moved the sign of the cross to Sunday following an opportunity of personal (private—in the context of the body of Christ) confession.

OTHER BOOKS BY THIS AUTHOR & THEIR THEMES

This is Terry's second paper back published book. He has eight e-published books. His themes and book titles are as follows.

Holiness
(Living into Holy—Love)

They are:

Confessional Holiness

...The Missing Piece of the Puzzle...

(A Theological and personal journey into following Jesus)

Millennial Holiness

... A post-modern invitation to Walk with Jesus...

(To live Jesus in community following him into the renewed earth that He is bringing)

Same Sex Marriage

...the last Prejudice?
...or the last righteous stand?
...or Both?

Terry has written several devotional books around the Liturgical Calendar of the Church. Five are currently e-published and available at Amazon.com as well; Two as yet are unwritten.

Devotional Journey's Around the Church's Calendar
(Making Holy—Love Real)

Advent

The Advent of God through Mary
…A Devotional Journey in the Christmas Season as seen through Mary's Eyes

Lent

Who Am I?
…Discovering Jesus through Lent
(A Journey with Jesus from a retreat center on Mount Herman to Mount Calvary)

Sundays of Easter

50 Days of Promise
…A journey from Easter to Pentecost

Ordinary Time

7 Faces of Jesus
…A devotional journey through the American Church

Jerusalem's Gates
…A devotional journey through the Gates of Jerusalem and into the Story of God

The next two books, yet to be written are:

Epiphany (Ordinary Time)
Down & Dirty
...A Narrative & Devotional Journey with Jesus in the Season of Epiphany

Ordinary Time
Generations: A Devotional Narrative about two Sisters & two Brothers
...A look into 'The Greatest Generation' and 'The Millennial Generation'

ABOUT THE AUTHOR
REV. TERRY MATTSON

Terry is an ordained elder in the Church of the Nazarene, having just completed an 18-year pastoral assignment at West Seattle Church of the Nazarene (WSCN). WSCN is a small multi-cultural and cross-generational and economic community historically focused on ministry among Native and Samoan tribal communities, the homeless and the nurturing of Gen-xers and now Millennials.

Prior to Seattle, Terry served in business administration and as youth and worship lay and paid staff in Nazarene churches in Omaha NE, Twin Falls ID and Vancouver WA.

Following high school and college, Terry has continued his interest in theological studies and reflection in classes with Pacific Rim School of Theology, Western Evangelical Seminary and in several still unpublished writings. Terry serves as an associate instructor/facilitator for Kaleidoscope, a Multicultural Learning Center of the Washington Pacific District Church of the Nazarene.

In all Terry's focus has been the cross over point between culture and holiness and in worship as formational in social and personal salvation…especially the 'human' inside The Story of God.

Find out more at: Terrys blog "Musings of a Pastor From a Place In-Between".

http://www.terrymattson-musingsofapastorfromapacein-between.directory/

Made in the USA
Las Vegas, NV
19 February 2023